THANK YOU FOR YOUR SERVICE

A Caughey Family Tribute

Lynne Caughey Holden

Thank You for Your Service
A Caughey Family Tribute

By

Lynne Caughey Holden

Visit our website at **www.StillwaterPress.com** for more information.

First Stillwater River Publications Edition

ISBN-10: 0-692-55601-X
ISBN-13: 978-0-692-55601-6

Library of Congress Control Number: 2015917059

1 2 3 4 5 6 7 8 9 10
Written by Lynne Caughey Holden
Photographs from the Caughey Family Collection. Reprinted with permission
Cover design by Dawn M. Porter.
Published by Stillwater River Publications, Glocester, RI, USA.

DEDICATION

This little volume is dedicated to all American veterans both past and present. We are grateful for their service to their country in times of peace and in times of war. We thank them for their service.

CONTENTS

INTRODUCTION

This book has grown out of a query from my grandson, Mark T. Holden, who was asked to bring a veteran to his elementary school to honor Veterans Day in November 2012. He asked his mother if he had a veteran that he could bring to school. His mother explained that there were many veterans on both sides of his family. His grandfather, Robert Poteete lived in Georgia, too far away to come to school in Rhode Island. His great grandfather, Edward L. Caughey, who had died, served in the Navy. Mark was very disappointed and felt left out. I asked if he could take photos of his great grandfather or grandfather or some memento such as a medal from the Spanish American War to school and would that count? The answer was,"No." That answer started me on this project of researching and writing about the veterans in the Caughey family. This project also led me to ask my Caughey cousins to write about their fathers, daughters and sons who have served as sailors and soldiers over the years. What began as "my" project to help my grandson has become "our" project for the edification of all our grandchildren and perhaps, someday, their grandchildren.

I thought the Caughey line might be the easiest line to follow since they emigrated here in the mid-19th century. The Holden line comes from Justinian Holden who set sail on 10 April 1634 from Ipswich, Suffolk, England on the *Elizabeth* and settled in Watertown,

Massachusetts.[1] Years later his descendants, Dr. William Holden and Captain Samuel Holden[2] fought in the Revolutionary War. The Mellott/Clark/ Moorhead families on my maternal side of the family also came to this country in the mid 1600's. Gideon Merlet/Melot set sail on 12 October 1662 from Holland on the *De Purmelander Kerck* with his wife and four children and first settled on Staten Island.[3] From his descendants and other familial lines came several Revolutionary War soldiers we could write about: John, Obadiah and Benjamin Mellott, Capt. James Clark, and Fergus Moorhead. Fergus was captured by the Indians near Indiana, Pennsylvania and he was taken to Quebec. He eventually walked to freedom from Quebec to New York to Carlisle, Pennsylvania.[4]

We have plenty of interesting stories we could tell about many of our ancestors, far too many for this one book. Thus, we will give thanks and remember the soldiers and sailors from just one ancestral line, James and Elizabeth Coulter Caughey who came to America

---

[1] Eben Putnam, *The Holden Genealogy Ancestry and Descendants of Richard and Justinian Holden and Randall Holden,* Vol. 1 (Boston, MA: n.p., 1923), p. 57.

[2] Daughters of the American Revolution (DAR) # A056915 and Sons of the American Revolution (S.A.R.) # 33797.

[3] Carl Boyer III, *Ship Passenger Lists New York and New Jersey (1600-1825)* (Self Published Newhall, CA 1978), p. 130.

[4] Colonel Richard W. Watson, Sesqui Background, "Fergus and Jane (White) Moorhead, Pioneers", *Indiana Evening Gazette,*[PA] February 26, 1953, Vol. 53, NO 164, p. 37.

about 1815. The book will help to celebrate the bicentennial of their arrival and to remember their descendants who have served in the Armed Services ever since.

ACKNOWLEDGMENTS

I wish to acknowledge the help I received from past generations who left letters, memorabilia, and their personal stories about our family veterans. I also wish to acknowledge all family members who have been so supportive of this project: siblings Ted, Nancy, and Martha; cousins Dan, David and Bob, niece Debra, first cousins once removed Jan and Chis and distant cousins Darwin and Miles. Lastly, but most importantly, I want to thank Phyllis for her continued support and encouragements.

I

CELEBRATING
THE BICENTENNIAL ARRIVAL
OF JAMES
AND ELIZABETH COULTER CAUGHEY

1815/1816

The bicentennial year of the arrival of James and Elizabeth Caughey is an educated guess. I have not been able to locate any emigration records of James and Elizabeth leaving Northern Ireland, possibly from County Down, nor have I located any immigration records, such as Passenger Lists, showing us when or where this couple entered the United States. According to an ancient Caughey Bible [5] we know that they were

---

[5] Holy Bible (Edinburgh, Scotland 1746) Flyleaf: Transcription by Daisy Maude McCormick Caughey. Marriage date of James and Elizabeth Coulter, their birth dates and the birth dates of their children are given. The location of this Bible was last noted in 1930 to be with a distant relative living in California.

married 24 October 1814 in Ireland. We know that their first child, William James Caughey, was born 11 July 1817 in Burgettstown, Washington County, Pennsylvania.[6] Four other children were born while James and Elizabeth lived in Burgettstown: Mary, born 29 Oct, 1818; Clement Paterson, born 3 November 1820; John, born 6 January 1823; and Robert Coulter, born 1828.

The 1820 Federal Census does not give us a true snapshot of the American population. The enumerators for the Federal 1820 census asked for the head of household, the number of free white males and free white females of different age categories; the number of persons to be naturalized; the number of persons engaged in agriculture, commerce, or manufacturing; the number of "colored" persons (sometimes in age categories); and the number of other persons except Indians. The first time we find a James Caughey in any Federal census, he was living in Smith Township, Washington County, Pennsylvania enumerated in 1820. [7] He and Elizabeth would be in their late twenties. Perhaps they had James' mother, Mary, living with

---

[6] Holy Bible (Edinburgh, Scotland 1746) William James Caughey was born in the year of our Lord July 11th 1817. William's place of birth is stated in the 1850 Federal Census as Pennsylvania.
1850 U.S. Census, Allegheny County, Pennsylvania, population schedule, Manchester Bough Precinct, West Manchester Post Office dwelling 227, family 227, p. 329, William J.Caughey; NARA microfilm publication M432, roll 744.
[7] 1820 U.S. Census, Washington County, Pennsylvania, population schedule, Smith Township, p. 217, James Caughey; NARA microfilm publication M33, roll 113.

them. Three people of the household worked in manufacturing, perhaps these three were James, Elizabeth and Mary. There is no way to be sure this is our James Caughey without the names of wife and children but a case can be made, especially since we know the above children were born in Burgettstown.

By the time of the 1830 Federal Census a James Caughey family was living in Allegheny City, Allegheny County, Pennsylvania.[8] The enumerators asked for similar information as the 1820 census. In 1830 there were additional persons who were under the age of 16. We know because of the family Bible, that Clement Paterson, John and Robert were old enough to be enumerated.

Three additional children were born into the household for the 1840 census: Milton Jay, 11 November 1832; Elizabeth, December 1835; and Anna F. June 1840.

James was a tailor in 1850.[9] He and his family were living in Manchester Borough, Allegheny County, Pennsylvania. The 1850 Federal Census now enumerates the names of everyone in the household so we can be very certain this is our James and Elizabeth. James

---

[8] 1830 U.S. Census, Allegheny County, Pennsylvania, population schedule Allegheny Township, p. 77, James Cauchey; NARA microfilm publication M 19, roll 144.

[9] 1850 U.S. Census, Allegheny Co., Pennsylvania, population schedule, Manchester Borough Precinct, West Manchester Post Office dwelling 306, family 306, p. 576 (penned) 334B (stamped). James Caughey; NARA microfilm publication M432, roll 744.

is 58 years old and he was born in Ireland. His real estate is valued at $1,000. Elizabeth is 55 and she was also born in Ireland. John, age 27 is a blacksmith; Robert, age 21, is a coach trimmer; Milton, age 18, is a coach maker; Elizabeth, age 15 and Annie, age 10 both attended school. All the children were listed as born in Pennsylvania. Three boarders lived with James and Elizabeth: a coach trimmer, a coach painter and a blacksmith. The oldest son, William, was enumerated with his household: his wife Susan and their six children. They were also living in Manchester Borough. William was a blacksmith.[10]

Only Robert, Milton and Ann were living at home with James and Elizabeth in 1860.[11] Elizabeth married the blacksmith, Joseph Young, on 28 December 1852.[12] Joseph was one of the young men living with the family in 1850.

Found in a survey of the early deeds of Allegheny County (Vol. 92, page 165) recorded on April 14, 1850 in the borough of Manchester, son John leased a piece of property for life to James and Elizabeth for the sum of one dollar yearly, to be paid on

---

[10] 1850 U.S. Census, Allegheny Co., Pennsylvania, population schedule, Manchester Borough Precinct, West Manchester Post Office dwelling and visitation 227, p. 329A. William J. Caughey; NARA mircrofilm publication M432, roll 744.
[11] 1860 U.S. Census, Allegheny Co., Pennsylvania, population schedule, Manchester Borough, dwelling 742, family 751, p. 401. James Caughey; NARA microfilm publication M653, Roll 1062.
[12] Pennsylvania, Marriages, 1852-1854, on line database at Ancestry.com, citing Pennsylvania State Archives; Reel 668.

January first. The property was on the corner of Chartier and Juniata Streets. James and Elizabeth were responsible for the maintenance, taxes and repairs. They lived in this home until 1864, when John and his wife, Sarah Jane, sold the property to Frederick Bollman, who in turn rented the home back to James and Elizabeth. James is always listed as a "gent" in the many issues of the <u>Directory of Pittsburgh and Allegheny Cities</u> from 1861-1875.

The death notice for James read:

"CAUGHEY-Wednesday morning, April 27, 1881, at 7:15 o'clock, James Caughey, in his 89th year. Funeral services at his late residence, Number 267 Magnolia Street, Allegheny, on Thursday morning, at 10 o'clock. Interment private at 2 o'clock P.M." <u>Pittsburgh Commercial Gazette</u>, Thursday, April 28, 1881."

James is buried in the Union Dale Cemetery, 2200 Brighton Road, Pittsburgh, PA Division One Lot 13 Range 4 Section M Grave #5. Elizabeth is buried alongside James in grave # 4. Elizabeth died 30 September 1882.[13] The couple had been married 67 years. Both died of "Old Age" according to the Registration of Deaths in the City of Allegheny. Allegheny City is now what is called the North Side of Pittsburgh.

The picturesque spot of Union Dale Cemetery where James and Elizabeth are buried, along with their son Robert and daughter Elizabeth Young and her

---

[13] Registration of Deaths in the City of Allegheny, State of Pennsylvania, A.D. 1882. Vol1: 111.

family, has a magnificent view of the skyline of the modern day Pittsburgh.

We can only speculate what brought James and Elizabeth to Pittsburgh in 1815 or 1816. Perhaps, Mary, James' mother, had preceded them to America. [14] Perhaps the couple was seeking a new start in a new country. Pittsburgh was a thriving industrial city in the early 1800s with many work opportunities. Many immigrants from Europe found work in the steel mills, iron, glass, and other factories along Pittsburgh's famous three rivers. Liza Alzo's, *Pittsburgh Immigrants,* pays tribute to the many hardworking men and women who made significant contributions to the growth and development of western Pennsylvania. [15]

In any case, James and Elizabeth Caughey and their children, grandchildren and beyond helped to fashion this city we all love. James and Elizabeth's children were bankers, blacksmiths, coach makers and coach trimmers. Their son, Clement Paterson, enlisted in the Union Army. Another son, Robert, held the city office of Burgess. He died an untimely death on Christmas Eve 1861 when he came to the aid of his neighbor whose house was aflame.[16] Their grandchildren and beyond have been, among other occupations: teachers, engineers, scientists, steel workers, glass manufacturers, state workers, secretaries, clergy, stock brokers, lawyers, automobile technicians, nurses, doctors, machinists,

---

[14] Email from Miles Caughey ,25 November 1999.

[15] Lisa A. Alzo. *Pittsburgh's Immigrants*, (Charleston, South Carolina, Arcadia Publishing, 2006), p. 7.

[16]"Tragedy Strikes" *Pittsburgh Gazette*, Pittsburgh, PA, Friday Morning, December 27, 1861.

shop keepers, soldiers and sailors. We salute and dedicate this book to the memory of James and Elizabeth
Coulter Caughey and their arrival to this country 200
years ago and to the great city of Pittsburgh, Pennsylvania.

A full geneaological chart of the descendants of James and
Elizabeth Coulter Caughey is in Appendix A.

James Caughey

Gravesite of James and Elizabeth Caughey

II

CLEMENT PATERSON CAUGHEY

1820-1899

RAGS TO RICHES - RICHES TO RAGS

Clement Paterson Caughey, known as C.P., was born 3 November 1820 in Burgettstown, Washington County, Pennsylvania, the third child of James and Elizabeth Coulter Caughey. According to a copy of his obituary, when C.P. was 14 years old, he and his family moved to Allegheny City, which is now part of the North Side of Pittsburgh. C.P. left his formal schooling when he was 14 and entered the mercantile house of George R. White, at Fourth Avenue and Market Street, Pittsburgh. He began as an office boy and eventually he became a manager for the firm.

The convergence of the three rivers of Pittsburgh: the Monongahela, Allegheny and the Ohio helped to make the city a thriving commercial center. By the early 1850s Pittsburgh was booming. While working at the firm of George R. White, C.P. had learned the ins and outs of commerce, investments and commercial trading. In his obituary we learn that at some point in the 1850s, C.P. had secured an interest in several steamboat lines on the Ohio and Missouri Rivers and he was financially very successful.

In the 1850 Federal Census,[17] C. P. is enumerated as a boarder living in Ward 2 of Pittsburgh. He was a clerk in a bank. By 1860 he was working for the banking house of Hanna, Hart & Company. He was well known in the financial circles of Pittsburgh and he was largely interested in coal, oil and gas properties.

He rented a home in 1860 in the First Ward of Pittsburgh. He was a banker with personal property valued at $4000.[18] Perhaps he lived at 61 Third Avenue when the 1860 was taken. We know he lived at 61 Third Avenue in 1861.[19] When researching the Pittsburgh Directories, published by George H. Thurston, from 1861- 1875, C.P. seems to have a new address each year. In 1875 he was living with his father, James, at 171 Juniata, Allegheny City. However, up to 1873, his place of employment was always listed as Hanna, Hart & CO. and he was always listed as a banker.

The U.S. IRS Tax Assessment Lists for the State of Pennsylvania, City of Pittsburgh enumerates

---

[17] 1850 U.S. Census, Allegheny Co., Pennsylvania, population schedule, Ward 2, Pittsburgh, p. 58, dwelling 66 , family 72 , C.P. Caughey; NARA microfilm publication M432, roll 745.
[18] 1860 U.S. Census, Allegheny Co., Pennsylvania, population schedule, Ward 2 Pittsbugh, p. 311, dwelling 1921, family 2465, C.P. Caughey; NARA microfilm publication M653, Roll 1058.
[19] Directory of Pittsburgh and Allegheny Cities 1861-1862 (George H. Thurston, 1861) p. 49 Caughey, C.P. of Hanna, Hart &CO., bds 61 Third.

the firm of Hanna, Hart &CO at 3rd and Wood Avenues of Pittsburgh. The principals of the firm were Joshua Hanna, W.K. Hart and C.P. Caughey. In 1862 the tax assessed to the firm was $50.00. In 1864, C.P.'s personal income and securities were taxed for $614.39 and in 1865 his total tax burden was $1396.10.[20] Much money was made during the period of the Civil War by Hanna, Hart & CO. During that time C.P. Caughey was making good money. His brief months of active service for the Union Army from April to August did not interrupt his banking and investment career. More will be written about his Army days in chapter III.

Black Friday, September 1873[21]

---

[20] Ancestry.com. U.S. IRS Tax Assessment Lists, 1862-1918 [database on line]. Provo, UT, USA: Ancerstry.com Operations Inc, 2008.

[21] http:// srnels.people.wm.edu/articles/realGrtDepr.html

C.P. remained in banking until 1873. It was during the financial panic of 1873 that his bank was among a number of banks "forced to the wall" and he and the bank were financially ruined. The crash of the banks and the Great Depression, which followed, not only in the United States, but throughout Europe, lasted four long years. The railroad companies faltered first and when Jay Cooke, the great railroad financier, was unable to pay his debts, the stock market crashed in September, closing hundreds of banks.

As the country was thrust into depression, countless families were financially destroyed and made homeless when mortgages could not be paid. People were out of work and many roamed the countryside looking for shelter, food and work. The terms "tramp" and "bum," indirectly referring to former Civil War soldiers, became commonplace American terms. Relief rolls exploded. Unemployed workers rioted in Boston, Chicago and New York in the winter of 1873-74 demanding public work. A nationwide railroad strike followed in 1877, in which mobs destroyed railway hubs in Pittsburgh, Chicago and Cumberland, Maryland. It was an awful time in history, and C.P. Caughey went from riches to rags: no job, no money, and alcohol became his comforter. Scott Reynolds Nelson, a professor of history at the College of William and Mary wrote, "…when banks fall on Wall Street, they stop all the traffic on Main Street-for a very long time."[22]

Following the failure of Hanna, Hart & CO., C.P. Caughey went to California to seek his fortune.

---

[22] http://srnels.people.wm.edu/articles/realGrtDepr.html

He did not stay long in California and returned to Pittsburgh where he became the toll collector on the Seventh Street Bridge. There he lived in a tiny toll booth shack at the end of the bridge, no longer listed in a Pittsburgh Directory, no longer a well-known figure in the financial world, rarely sober and of no interest to the IRS. By 1890 he was employed as a night watchman for the Pittsburgh Safe Deposit Company.[23] It is interesting to note that I found only one piece of evidence to mark the time C.P. spent in California. *The Oakland Daily Evening Tribune*, dated Wednesday, August 4, 1875 gave a list of passengers who had arrived by overland train that evening, and a Mrs. C.P. Caughey from Pennsylvania was named![24]

I don't know if his marriage survived his financial ruination. The only record that he had married is in the 1880 Census. In the 1880 U.S. Census he and his wife, Rose, age 35 were living at 219 Washington Avenue, 6th Ward, Allegheny City, Allegheny County, Pennsylvania. They had four children: Clement P.. age 6; John, age 5; Alexander N., age 3 and Saddie, age 9 months. Saddie (Sarah) was born in September. C.P. was employed as a clerk in

---

[23] Pittsburgh City Directory, 1890, (Pittsburgh, Pa . J.F. Diffenbacher) CP Caughey Safe Deposit Co. night guard.

[24] http:// www.newspapers.com/imagine/66513465. Overland Arrivals To-night, "Following is a list of passengers to arrive by overland train this evening", *Oakland daily Evening Tribune,* [CA] August 4, 1875, Vol.VI, NO 435, p. 3.

a forge. A niece, Odessa Caughey, age 15, was also living with them.[25]

There is no 1890 census record of Clement Paterson Caughey, born 3 November 1820. I have found no death record. The Pennsylvania Veterans Burial Cards, 1777-1999 proved to be very helpful by giving me the date of his death as 26 January 1899. He was buried in Highwood Cemetery on Brighton Road, North Side, Pittsburgh, PA. in Section Q, Lot No.145. Also noted on this form was that P. Clement Caughey was a veteran of the Civil War. His dates of service were from 25 April 1861 to 5 August 1861. Army Co. B, 11th PA. Volunteers: Rank Sergeant.

There is an error on the *Record of Burial Place of Veteran*, stating that C.P. Caughey served in the 11th Regiment. C.P. served with the 12th Regiment of Company B Pennsylvania Volunteers.[26]

Highwood Cemetery, Pittsburgh, PA

---

[25] 1880 U.S. Census, Allegheny County., Pennsylvania, population schedule, 6th Ward Allegheny City, p. 580A, Clement P. Caughey; NARA microfilm publication T9, Roll: 1087.
[26] http:// www.findagrave.com Sgt Clement P. Caughey

III

THE AMERICAN CIVIL WAR

1861 - 1865

The American Civil War began on 12 April 1861 when South Carolina troops fired on Fort Sumter in Charlestown Harbor. On April 19th President Lincoln ordered a blockade of the ports of South Carolina, Georgia, Alabama, Florida, Mississippi, Louisiana, and Texas and this proclamation was the declaration of war by the Union against the Confederacy. The Civil War is also referred to by some historians as, "The War between the States," the "War of Succession," the "War of Northern Aggression," and the "War for the Suppression of the Rebellion."

Approximately 3.5 million soldiers fought in the war resulting in over 600,000 deaths.

Military Service

Clement P. Caughey was Fourth Sergeant of Company B of the 12th Regiment. He was mustered into the Army on 25 April 1861 and mustered out on

1 August 1861. He served under Captain John S. Kennedy.[27] According to the Pennsylvania State Archives, "Civil War Veteran's Card File," C.P. was 35 years old when he answered President Lincoln's call for volunteer soldiers.[28] Maybe C.P. was less than honest about his age because he was anxious to serve or maybe the recorder at his time of service was wrong about his age. C.P.'s tombstone has his birth year as 1820, as does the record found in the Caughey Family Bible. If his birthdate is 1820 then he was 41 years old when he enlisted.

He was recruited in Pittsburgh, Pennsylvania and he was sent to Harrisburg, PA where he was sworn in and commissioned as sergeant. Governor Curtin of Pennsylvania reviewed the troops and the men were moved to York, PA by train as part of General Patterson's Department of Pennsylvania. One month later, C.P. and Company B were assigned guard duty for the Northern Central Railroad from the Pennsylvania state line to Baltimore, MD. The headquarters for the Company was at Cockeysville, MD.[29] Securing the railroads was important to the Union Army for supply lines and troop transportation. C.P. was stationed in Cockeysville for three months and he returned to Pittsburgh and to his banking career.

---

[27] Pennsylvania Volunteers of the Civil War http://www.pacivilwar.com/cwpal2b.html.

[28] Civil War Veterans card File, 1861-1866. http://www.digitalarchives.state.pa.us/archives.asp?view.

[29] Civil war in the East. http://www.civil-warintheeast.com/USA/PA/PA012.php.

During the Civil War, flags played an important part on every battlefield. They were the heart and soul of every regiment. Even though Company B of the 12th Regiment did not see battle, their flag would still be very important to the morale of the men. Had the Company been in battle, the flag would be a rallying point when the regiment became disorganized. A usual command was for the men to "close on colors," and when the advance faltered, the colonel would order, "advance the colors" to inspire the men to follow their flag.[30]

I was unable to find a photograph of the 12th Regiment infantry flag. However, I did find the 11th Regiment Infantry Flag which may have been similar to the 12th Regiment.[31]

Photo of 11th regiment flag

---

[30] Pennsylvania Volunteers of the Civil War
http://www/pacivilwar.com/cwpaflags.html.
[31] Pennsylvania Volunteers of the Civil War -Civil War Flags.
http://www.pacivilwarflags.org/regiments/regiment-List.cfm?group=1-50.

Allegheny County Soldiers & Sailors Memorial Hall

Twelfth Regiment Pennsylvania Volunteers

Tablet #51 Sergeants - Clement P. Caughey

From C.P.'s obituary:

"…He was a member of the 12th PA volunteers during the War of the Rebellion and at one time was Lieutenant of Company B of the Duquesne Grays." The Duquesne Grays were a National Guard Unit stationed in Pittsburgh.

C.P. filed for a Civil War pension on 11 July 1895. His rank, company and regiment are given. His enlistment and discharge listed. His application number, as an invalid, is 1168656. His death is annotated as Jan 25, 1899.[32]

Our final glimpse of C.P. and his military service can be found on the Roll of Honor, Tablet number 51, at the Allegheny County Soldiers', Sailors' and Marines' Memorial on Fifth Avenue and Bigelow Boulevard, Pittsburgh, PA.[33]

---

[32] The Organization Index to Pension Files of Veterans Who Served Between 1861 and 1900. NARA, T289; Roll 457. Caughey, Clement P. http://www.footnote.com/imagine/5909677/caughey.

[33] Evans, Samuel M. *Allegheny County, Pennsylvania, in the War for the Suppression of the Rebellion*, 1861-1865: roll of honor, defenders of the flag, attack on Fort Sumter, S.C. April 12, 1861, surrender at Appomattox, VA., April 9, 1865. Pittsburgh, University of Pittsburgh, Digital Research Library, 1999. p. 86.

Obituary (from unknown source)

Clement Patterson Caughey, age 79 years, at one time a prominent banker of Pittsburgh, died yesterday at his residence after a short illness of pneumonia. He was a native of Burgettstown, PA (Washington Co) where he was born 3 Nov 1820. He came to Pittsburgh when only 14 years old and entered the mercantile house of George R. White, at Fourth Avenue and Market Street, where he remained for a number of years, rising from office boy to manger. Early in the 1850's Mr. Caughey secured an interest in several steamboat lines on the Ohio and Missouri Rivers, in which business he was very successful. Later he entered the banking house of Palmer, Hanna & Company. He became well known in the financial circles and was largely interested in coal, oil and gas properties, in which he made large sums of money. In the financial panic of 1873 his bank was among a number forced to the wall, and he was ruined financially. After that he went to California, but returned to Pittsburgh. He became a toll collector on the Seventh Street Bridge, and later acted as watchman for the Pittsburgh Safe Deposit Company. He was a member of the 12th PA volunteers during the War of the Rebellion and at one time was Lieutenant of Company B of the Duquesne Grays. He is survived by five sons and two daughters, as follows: C.P. Caughey, Alexander Nimick Caughey, John and B.M. Caughey; and Fanie A. and Sarah A. Caughey.[34]

---

[34] Copy of Obituary from Personal Email 25 Nov 1999 from Miles A. Caughey, Jr.

My great-granduncle had an extraordinary life and truly went from rags to riches and riches to rags. We honor him and his three month service to preserving the United States of America. His direct ancestral line continued in his service tradition.

C.P.'s great grandson, Miles A. Caughey, Jr. served for 43 years in the Army: 32 active and 11 years in the Reserves. He served in Korea, Iraq and Afghanistan. Miles' father, Miles A. Caughey, Sr. was in the Army Technical Support Group (TSG) in WWII and a Lt. in Korea. Miles A, Sr.'s brother, Clement Caughey, Jr. served as a sailor in WWII. [35]

---

[35] Personal Email 3 Feb 2015 from Miles A. Caughey, Jr.

IV

THE SPANISH AMERICAN WAR AND JOHN STEVENS CAUGHEY

"A Splendid Little War" - Statement made by John Hays, Secretary of State, William McKinley Administration[36]

When the U.S. battleship, *"Maine"* mysteriously exploded and sank in the Havana Harbor, Cuba on 15 February 1898, John and many other Americans knew that war between Spain and the U.S. was imminent. Everyone knew the rallying cry, "Remember the Maine." Americans sympathized with the Cubans who were fighting for their independence from Spain. Tempers were rising in Congress and President William McKinley declared war on Spain on 20 April 1898. On April 27th John Stevens Caughey, my grandfather, enlisted in the Pennsylvania National Guard, joining the Light Battery B, artillery unit.

---

[36] http://history.state.gov/milestones/1866-1898/spanish-american-war.

John Stevens was living with his parents, John and Sarah, in Allegheny City, Allegheny County, Pennsylvania.[37] Today that area is called the North Side of Pittsburgh. John was 23 years old. His sister, Mary Elizabeth, was contracted to be a nurse and his brothers, Samuel Neal and Clement Patterson also enlisted. John's parents had four of their children involved in this "splendid little war."

What a worry that must have been. No one at the time of enlistment knew that this war would be over in seven months. When peace was declared the United States had annexed Hawaii, claimed the Philippine Islands, Guam, and Puerto Rico and had liberated Cuba.

John, along with 16 officers and 67 men left for Mount Greta, PA to be sworn in as recruits into the United States Army. There they remained until May 18th and, under orders from the War Department, reported to Camp Thomas in Chickamauga, Georgia. [38] The following photographs were taken while John was stationed at Camp Thomas.

---

[37] Ancestry.com. Pennsylvania, Spanish War Compensation, 1898-1934 [database on-line]. Provo, UT.

[38] Steward, Adj. Gen. Thomas J., Record of the Pennsylvania Volunteers. (Harrisburg: William Stanley Ray, 1901) p. 771-773.

John Stevens Caughey, soldier

Left: John Stevens Caughey, Sr. 1823-1904 - father of John Stevens Caughey and Right: Sarah Jane Harper 1836-1914 - mother of John Stevens Caughey

The Battery stayed at Camp Thomas until July 16 when it was ordered to Newport News, Virginia where the men embarked on the transport ship *"Roumania"* for Puerto Rico on July 27th. This ship originally carried cattle making the passage to Puerto Rico most unpleasant in ways of creature comforts for the soldiers and the smells were awful! There was never a question about using this ship for cattle, yet someone in the government or army gave no thought to the use of this ship for soldiers. When water leaked into the sleeping quarters the floors turned to foul muck. How dreadful for these men of Battery B.

Their ship ran aground off the port of Guanica on the southern coast of Puerto Rico. The battery disembarked and twelve hours later they were afloat again and bound for Ponce to report to General Mills. After landing in Ponce, orders were received for the ship to proceed to Arroyo, Puerto Rico arriving August 4th. A detail of the battery had to build a wharf for unloading purposes and a detail had to build a bridge over a creek on the road to Guayana. Which detail John was assigned is not known, but it would be the first time that he was exposed to the heat, mosquitoes, and tropical jungles. The bridge was 85 feet long and "substantially" made.[39]

John and his battery made camp at Arroyo and they stayed there one week until the forward movement to Guayana began and they occupied the city on August 12th. Not a shot was fired and the city welcomed the Americans who had come to liberate them from the Spanish. On the evening of August 13th the Americans began their movement toward El Cayey. Here the Spanish were entrenched. They were directed to put in an action front by Major General Brooke.

Traveling with Battery B was a famous newspaper correspondent, Richard Harding Davis. He described the battle preparations as follows:

"The shell was in the chamber; the gunner aimed the piece and had run backward, but before it spoke, Lieutenant MacLaughlin, of the Signal Corps, galloped upon the scene shrieking, 'Cease firing, peace has been declared!'

Whereat the men swore."[40]

---

[39] Ibid.

[40] McSherry, Patrick. <u>A Brief History of Pennsylvania Volunteer Artillery, Light Battery B.</u> (<u>http://www</u>. Span-amwar.com/PABattery B. htm)

The battle never occurred. The war, for John, consisted only of battle preparations, and difficult sea travels. One hundred seventy three enlisted men and officers, along with those in the enemy lines, were spared a bloody conflict. Men would have been killed and maimed, families destroyed and broken hearted had a battle occurred. Maybe John would have been killed and that would have been the end of my direct family line. There would have been military horses and mules killed or maimed. John and his fellow battery volunteers were spared the unseen emotional and psychological battle scars. The unit suffered one loss of an enlisted man, and that was attributed to disease.[41] Typhoid and yellow fever killed more soldiers, nurses and other military personnel than the actual fighting.

John was a witness to this pivotal point of the war with Spain. The Peace Protocol was signed in Washington and all hostilities ended. On September 2nd all transportation, horses, harnesses, mules, and wagons were turned over to the Quartermaster's Department and the unit embarked on the ship *"Concho"* and left Ponce. The ship arrived in New York City on September 15th. It had been a rough voyage with much sea sickness due to the foul weather. Pennsylvania Governor Hastings greeted the men and John was able to come home to an enthusiastic welcome in Pittsburgh on September 18th. He was mustered out of the battery in November 1898.

---

[41] ibid

Supply carts in Puerto Rico

Tombstone of John Stevens Caughey

The last public mention of John Stevens Caughey's military service was in the Sewickley *Herald* newspaper for the Memorial Day celebrations in 1942, the year I was born. A photo of the men from the Pittsburgh and Sewickley area of Battery B taken in 1898 was featured on the front page. [42]

---

[42] The Herald, The Sewickley Valley's Home News Weekly. May 28, 1942, Vol. 39. No. 24, p. 1.

John was not the only member of the Caughey family of note in the "splendid little war." John's brother, Samuel Neal Caughey served as a private in the 14th Regiment, Pennsylvania Infantry and Mary Elizabeth, John's sister, was a contract nurse for the Army. This was the first time the government sought out a civilian female organization to help with the war efforts. The government asked the DAR (Daughters of the American Revolution) to contact, contract, and organize nurses for the military. These nurses were eventually recognized as members of the military and Mary Elizabeth, like her brothers, received a pension for her military service. John was on the battlefield on that historic day that peace was declared. Mary and other contract nurses, made history by being made the first official female Army veterans. This "splendid little war," ended Spain's colonial presence in the Caribbean granting independence to Cuba and securing American power and interests in the Pacific with the annexation of Hawaii and the control of the Philippines and Guam. This war enabled Teddy Roosevelt, made famous with his leadership of the Rough Riders in Cuba, to further his career to become President of the United States. I suppose one can say much was accomplished with this "splendid little war."

"Remember the Maine"

and

Remember the Contract Nurses of the Spanish American War!

Mary Elizabeth Caughey, RN 1872-1967

Mary Elizabeth Caughey was my paternal great aunt who was recruited and served as a contract nurse during the Spanish American War. The Daughters of the American Revolution (DAR) were directly responsible for my great-aunt's service: a chapter in her life's story of which she was immensely proud. She was a lady short in stature, but a giant in compassion for others through her nursing skills.

Battling typhoid fever, dysentery, malaria, and yellow fever in the military camps of 1898 made paramount the need for trained nurses. Diseases were causing ten times the deaths as battle injuries and these deaths almost lost the war for the United States. The Army had trained male medical personnel but there were not enough of these nurses to meet the overwhelming needs for the 28,000- man Army. Despite the attempt to recruit another 6,000 male nurses there simply were not enough men who qualified as trained nurses.[43]

Into the trenches stepped Dr. Anita Newcomb McGee, physician and Vice-President General of the

---

[43] Stieham, Judith Hicks, Ed. It's Our Military, Too! Women and the U.S. Military. (Philadelphia: Temple University, Press, 1996) p. 88.

Daughters of the American Revolution. She volunteered her organization to help fill the need for trained female nurses. Naturally, there were reservations about having women serving in the field with male soldiers. But need overcame reservations! On 28 April 1898 Congress granted authority to the Surgeon General to appoint female nurses on contract. Dr. McGee was appointed Assistant Surgeon General to screen nurse applications.[44] Through Dr. McGee's work, and the volunteers of the DAR, over 5,000 applications from across the nation were examined. "To qualify, nurses had to be graduates of a recognized training school and be between the ages of 30 and 50. They were to provide character recommendations and take an oath of allegiance to the United States. The DAR Hospital Corps certified 1,081 thoroughly trained women for service at the front."[45] Mary Elizabeth Caughey was one of those certified, trained nurses.

Mary Elizabeth, often called "Mollie," was 26 years old when she enlisted 28 August 1898. There is no record to show how Mary was able to be certified at the age of 26 years, but she was and she served at Fort McPherson, Atlanta, Georgia. She was recruited by the DAR and served until February 28, 1899. The Army Hospital at Fort McPherson was a 922 bed facility and many of the soldiers were treated for the tropi-

---

[44] Spanish American War Nurses. (Women in Military Service for the America Memorial Foundation, Inc. Arlington, VA. 1951) 35.

[45] Supplement to American Spirit Magazine. (Washington DC) Vol 14, No. 6, November/December 2014, p. 436.

cal diseases of yellow fever and malaria, along with dysentery and typhoid, the last two prevalent in overcrowded conditions.

After the war, Mary Elizabeth returned home to Allegheny City, Pittsburgh in 1899. By 1900 she and her family had moved from Pittsburgh to Old Economy Village, Harmony Township, Beaver County, PA. She and her parents, John and Sarah, along with brothers John Steven and Samuel Neal were enumerated as living on Main Street in the 1900 Federal Census.[46]

Mary had an unhappy marriage to Attorney Lewis M. Shaffer. They had married in 1906 and there is no Caughey, living or dead, who said or who will say, a good word about this man who was cruel to his wife and his animals. In applications for a pension from her service during the war, Mary wrote she was "married by a minister" and made no mention of her divorce. In later papers for her pension she wrote she was now a widow.

Mary spent the rest of her working career as a private duty nurse to various members, and extended members, of the family. She lived with her sister, Alice Caughey Luty on 719 Thorne Street in Sewickley, PA from 1929-1944.[47] In 1945 she moved to 716 Broad Street, Sewickley to live with her sister-in-law, and my

---

[46] 1890 Federal Census Harmony Township, Beaver County, Economy Village, PA. T623 roll 1374, Vol 32, ED 33, Sheet 4A and Line 28.

[47] 1930 Federal Census Sewickley Borough, Allegheny County, PA. T626_1990, ED 2-487, Sheet 4B, Line 83.

1940 Federal Census Sewickley, Allegheny, PA: Roll T627_3416. ED 2-487, p. 6B.

grandmother, Maude McCormick Caughey, then, widow of John Stevens.

On July 25, 1950 Mary moved into Miller Cottage at the Veterans Administration Center, 4100 West Third Street, Dayton, Ohio. She lived for 17 years at the Veteran Center. This is where I would go with my father to visit with her. My father was the youngest child of John and Maude to whom she was devoted, and she took a special delight in her nephew, Edward. Mary's Army pension from her service as a contract nurse was $90. Her pension number was C #2-593-160.[48] Without the help of the DAR and Dr. Anita McGee, Mary and many other contract nurses would not have qualified for an Army Pension.

After the Spanish American War, Dr. McGee and the DAR campaigned and petitioned the Army and Congress to recognize the service of the contract nurses Dr. McGee had supervised. In 1901 Congress granted military status to the contract nurses and the Army Nurse Corp was officially formed.[49]

In spite of official recognition of Mary's military service and the fact that she received a military pension while she lived for 17 years at a veteran's facility, Mary was not granted a Spanish American tombstone or a Spanish American War marker.

---

[48] General Index to Pension Files, 1861-1934. Washington, D.C.: National Archives and Records administration. T288, 546 rolls.

[49] Spanish American War Nurses. p. 35.

Mary deserves her due. She served her country during the Spanish American War, as did her brothers, John, Neal and Paterson. All four siblings received military pensions. The brothers have military tombstones and grave markers for "the splendid little war." [50] "Remember the Maine," and remember Mary Elizabeth Caughey, registered nurse, who served those afflicted with disease and battle wounds from the Spanish American War.

Mary Elizabeth as a young woman

---

[50] http://history.state.gov/milestones/1866-1898/spanish-american-war "A splendid little war" was coined by John Hays, Secretary of State, under the William McKinley Administration.

V

THE SPANISH AMERICAN WAR AND SAMUEL N. CAUGHEY

PENNSYLVANIA INFANTRY
OCTOBER 5, 1873 - FEBRUARY 16, 1959

My grandfather's brother, Samuel Neal Caughey, was living in Middletown, Pennsylvania in the 1950s when I knew him. Above the fireplace was a sword and scabbard which he had issued to him during the Spanish American War. He walked with a severe limp using two heavy canes. My cousin, David G. Caughey, in private correspondence wrote:

"Uncle Neal had bad hips. He walked slowly and painfully with a cane--at least when I knew him. The story I heard was that he was standing on top of a boxcar and was shot at. He jumped and landed driving the femurs up into the hip socket. It happened in Puerto Rico, I guess."

Granduncle Neal's wife, Laura, was my grandmother's sister. The two Caughey brothers, John and

Samuel Neal married two McCormick sisters, Daisy and Laura, making them brothers and brothers-in-law and the same with the sisters. Their children were double first cousins. John and Neal were not only brothers but they were also business partners. They owned the milk company, JS Caughey &Bro,[51] at 412 Beaver Street, Sewickley, PA and later changed the name to The Sanitary Milk Company, a dairy business dealing with Milk, Eggs, and Butter.[52] By this time both brothers had married, their father had died and their mother came to live with them. It has been told that Daisy once said that Sarah was a very difficult person to live with, much less like. In my father's 1935 Sewickley High School Yearbook, *The Sewihi*, one will find an advertisement for the Sanitary Milk Company and the J.S. Caughey Restaurant.

Throughout the 1930s the Neal Caughey's lived in Haysville, Pennsylvania across the railroad tracks from my Dad's home on Dawson Avenue in

---

[51] 1905 DIRECTORY of the Residents, Business and Professional Men of Ambridge and Sewickley. R.L. Polk & Co. and R.L. Dudley
 p. 236
Caughey, John S. (J S Caughey &Bro), h 412 Beaver.
CAUGHEY J S & BRO (JOHN S and SAMUEL N), Dairy Products 412 Beaver, Bell 'phone Swky 294.
Caughey, Samuel N (J C Caughey & Bro), h 412 Beaver.

[52] 1908 DIRECTORY/Sewickley. R.L.Polk & Co. and R.L. Dudley, p. 291
Caughey John (Daisy), milk, h 212 Henry av.
Caughey Neal (Laura), milk, bds 212 Henry av.
Caughey Sarah (wid John), bds 212 Henry av.

Glenfield. Both communities used the Sewickley High School for their children. My father, Edward, son of John and Daisy enjoyed visiting with his uncle and aunt at River Road and he was very close to his cousins, Virginia and Sam.

During the Spanish American War, Neal enlisted on 27 April 1898 and served two years as a private of Company C of the 14th Regiment of Pennsylvania Volunteers, U.S. Infantry. He was "mustered out of the company" on 28 February 1899, in Summerville, S.C. On his discharge papers he was listed as 19 years old, 5 feet 7 1/2 inches with dark complexion, brown eyes and brown hair. The remarks on his discharge papers read: Service "honest and faithful"; Physical condition "good"; Character "Excellent." He was listed as a dairy man by occupation. [53] He filed for a military pension on June 25, 1929. His pension number was C2583278.[54]

According to Thomas J. Stewart's *The Record of the Pennsylvania Volunteers,* the 14th Regiment of Pennsylvania never left the United States. Stewart writes that the 14th Regiment was composed of eight companies, all from the city of Pittsburgh and other National Guard Units from Allegheny County. The regiment

---

[53] Government Discharge Paper, held in private, Titled To "All Whom it May Concern," stating Samuel N. Caughey's enlistment dates, his discharge dates, physical characteristics.

[54] Organization Index to Pension Files of Veterans Who Served Between 1861 and 1900. NARA, Pennsylvania, T289, Roll 521. www.footnote.com/image/22081107/caughey

was mustered in at Mt. Gretna, PA and several companies, including Company C were sent to Fort Mott, NJ. In September 1898 the Regiment was sent to Camp George G. Meade at Middletown, PA. It was at Camp Meade in Middletown that the "command participated in the Peace Jubilee Celebration in the City of Philadelphia, October 27, 1898."[55] The Regiment was sent to Summerville, South Carolina and was mustered out from Summerville on 28 February 1898. When Neal was celebrating the end of the Spanish American War in Middletown, PA, his brother, John, was leaving the "almost" battle at El Cayey, Puerto Rico. Neal's hip injuries may have happened while he was in uniform for the 14th Regiment, but those injuries happened somewhere in the States. Nevertheless, Neal answered the call to serve his country at a time when no one ever expected the "Splendid Little War" to be over almost before it began.

Neal and his wife, Laura, and son, Sam lived in Haysville, Allegheny County, Pa in 1930 and 1940 according to the Federal Census of those years. Their daughter, Virginia, married George Inskeep Morrow on 30 November 1933. They were married in Sewickley and moved to Middletown, PA. After the death of George in 1945, Laura and Neal went to Middletown to live with Virginia and her daughter Patricia.

Both Laura and Neal are buried in the Middletown Cemetery, Middletown, PA Lot 74-Dn (New); grave 1-C. Their marker reads:

---

[55] Steward, Adj. Gen. Thomas J., <u>Record of the Pennsylvania Volunteers.</u> (Harrisburg: William Stanley Ray, 1901) p. 570-571.

Caughey

| **Laura McCormick** | **Samuel Neal** |
| **1878-1965** | **1878-1959** |

A separate veteran marker reads:

Samuel N. Caughey
Pennsylvania
Pvt 14 Regt PA infantry
Spanish American War
October 5 1873 February 16 1959

A metal Spanish American marker is also at the grave.

Neal's Obituary from The " Middletown Journal," Thursday, February 19, 1959 page 5.

Samuel N. Caughey, *80, of 145 Race Street, died Sunday night at his home.*

He is survived by his wife, Mrs. Laura McCormick Caughey; a daughter, Mrs. Virginia Morrow, Middletown, a son Samuel N., Sewickley, and a granddaughter.

He was a member of St. Peter's Lutheran Church.

Services were held yesterday, Wednesday, from Reber Funeral Home, Spring and Waters Streets. Rev. Dr. Paul R. Clouser, pastor, officiated. Burial was in Middletown Cemetery.

Lot 74 Dn (new) Grave 1-C

Laura's Obituary "The Press and Journal" Middletown, PA Thursday January 6, 1966 sec 1 page 3.

Mrs. Laura Caughey

Mrs. Laura McCormick Caughey died Friday at Harrisburg Hospital. She resides with her daughter, Mrs. George Morrow, 145 Race St., Middletown.

Mrs. Caughey was a member of the St. Peter's Lutheran Church, Middletown. She was a teacher in the Ambridge (Pa) schools for a number of years and was postmistress at Haysville, Pa, at one time.

In addition to her daughter, she is survived by a son Neal Caughey, Sewickley, a granddaughter and great-granddaughter.

Services were held Monday at the Reber Funeral Home at Spring and Waters Sts., Middletown. Her pastor, the Rev. Richard E. Geib, officiated. Burial was in Middletown Cemetery.

Lot 74 Dn (new) Grave 2-C

Samuel N. Caughey

VI

A TRIBUTE TO THOSE WHO WAIT

MY GRANDMOTHER'S TREASURE BOX

An Interview with Daisy Maude McCormick Caughey through letters.

"Grandma; What is this box?" And this is her answer, written sometime in 1953:

> *"This was once a beautiful little casket now filled with precious letters of dear ones now gone when I shall soon rejoin them-and a few from ones still here and very dear. If my boys or sister should wish to read them they are welcome.*
>
> *Some are such precious letters from papa and mother and some from my dear John. The casket I won as a school prize. The only ones* (letters) *from Bob and Jack from school age.*
>
> *Also my letters from three persons required when I entered training.*
>
> *Have read all just before my 80th birthday*

I am in possession of The Treasure Box, or casket, as Grandmother called it. I expect it looks about the same as it did in 1953 when Grandmother had turned 80: well worn, shabby, something one would throw away if one did not take the time to investigate its contents. The Box measures 7.5 x 5 x 4.5 inches. The fabric that once covered this box was green tapestry fabric but today the base threads are all that are left of an elegant fabric and a few fuzzy, smooth nubs of threads. There was once a metal clasp and lock, yet the handle and filigree ornamentations on the corners show how fancy this box once was. It is now quite homely, and I think of the well-loved, Velveteen Rabbit. It is filled with the treasure of 81 letters.

"Grandma; what are the earliest letters that you saved and from whom?"

There is a letter dated July 23, 1894 to Miss Daisy McCormick. It has no envelope or postage mark as do most of the letters saved in The Treasure Box. This letter of 1894 begins,

Dear Granddaughter,

Your welcome letter received and will try to Scribble a few lines to you although in the very depth of loneliness very dark and cloudy raining a little there is nothing of importance to write…..John and family get along they don't write to me. I think sometimes that times are getting to hard for me to write but I can't give it up…..I would like so much to go and see you all if it is the Lord's will that my health will admit of it. I think so much about it that

sometimes I think I can go but don't know yet,
was sorry to hear of Laura being sick but hope
she is better now.

There is no signature on this letter as this is the only piece of paper dated 1894. Because the grandmother who is writing mentions John and family, this must mean that the author is Nancy Jane McFarland McCormick, mother of Robert M. McCormick, grandmother's father. John would be grandmother's uncle. Nancy Jane was born in Mifflin County, Pennsylvania (PA) 18 May 1820 and she died in Clarion County, PA 12 May 1896.

The other early letter is dated December 24, 1899 from Economy, PA

Dear Daughter Your letter was rec'd last
evening… I got you a very nice gold stick pin
with an opal set for a Christmas present it
seems a very poor return for all you give us but
with it goes my love to best Christmas wishes.
I hope you will like it… Clair, bless his dear
heart says there is not a drop of selfish blood
in your being, he appreciates his present…
now dear good night your mother.

Mother was Susan Blanche Stoughton McCormick. She was born in Clarion County 1 March 1847 and she died 3 November 1912 in Linesville, Crawford, PA.

Maude McCormick Caughey

"What was your courtship like, Grandma?"

Envelope postal mark Economy Jan 30 1901.

Caughey	2 cent stamp
And	
Ueckerman	Miss Maude McCormick
Dairymen	Fisher
Economy	Clarion Co., Pa.

My Dear Daisy

Did not get a letter from you this morning. I suppose the men are logging, and you couldn't make connections with the Post Office. However I will very likely get one in the morning and I do hope it will contain the good news I have waited so long to hear.

I think I will come up Saturday week weather (sic) you are ready to come home or not. I cannot wait much longer to see you.

We have nearly enough snow now for sleighing; it has been snowing a little all day...

Now Dade please write and tell me you will be ready to come home by Monday Feb 11th and I will come up Saturday Feb 9th, if you don't I will very likely be up anyway.

As ever

Jack

Same type of envelope

Economy Pa Feb 24 1901

My Dear Girl

This time last week you and I were curled up on the lounge in the kitchen and I was the happiest man on earth. It seems almost a life time since I was in Clarion. The time has gone slower the last few days than it has for years. And to think Darling it will be more than a week yet before I see you…

I hope your patient is getting on nicely and nothing will prevent you getting home. My Dear Girl my love for you grows stronger every day. I don't know what would happen if I would have to give you up. I prefer death a hundred times, rather than live without you…

Don't stay any longer than it is necessary, as a very impatient boy is waiting to welcome you home.

Give my love to all, and be sure and come home soon.

Jack

Economy, Pa March 6, 1901

My Dear Daisy,

Just returned from Washington D.C. late last evening.....I went with the Battery and it didn't cost me a dime…

My trip to Washington was simply to kill time, it seems to go so slow. However it must come to an end sometime, please don't extend the time any longer. I know I am selfish, but when consumed I can't help it…

As ever, Jack

There are seventeen loving and beseeching letters from Jack to Daisy and five post cards sent from Washington, D.C. The letters saved begin on January 4th and the last letter is dated March 6, 1901.

1942 - John and Daisy McCormick Caughey with Lynne Caughey

Daisy was a trained nurse. She had graduated from Allegheny General Hospital in Pittsburgh on 15 May 1900. My grandmother was most often employed as a Private Duty Nurse and from these seventeen letters I gathered that her patient in Fisher, Clarion County, PA was not mending as quickly as Jack wished. I also learned that my grandfather signed his letters, "Jack" but I have only heard him referred to as John or Dad.

John Stevens Caughey and Daisy Maude McCormick wed at the bride's home in Old Economy, PA on 10 September 1901.

In The Treasure Box there is a total of 81 letters, most with their accompanying envelop. There are letters from John Caughey's parents, John and Sarah; Daisy's parents, Robert and Blanche; Daisy's sisters, Edna and Laura; Daisy's brothers, St.Clair, known as Clair and Robert Lee; cousin Margaret, and Daisy's children, Bob and Jack. The post marks range from Economy, Sewickley, Titusville, and Linesville, PA, but also Dixon, IL; Sonora, TX; Jasper, AL; Boulder, CO; Muskogee, OK; Portland, OR; and one letter from Alaska. What I learned from these many sources is that between the years 1911 and 1913, Daisy's husband, John, her father, Robert, her brothers Robert Lee and Clair and her in-laws, John and Sarah were moving around the country in search of work in the newly discovered enterprise of drilling for oil. Clair McCormick stayed in Texas and was eventually employed by the Gulf Oil Company. While the family was on the move, Daisy and her children, Robert, John, and Paul stayed with her mother-in-law, Nancy McCormick, in Linesville, PA. All the letters dated within 1911 and 1913 were addressed to Mrs. J.S. Caughey Linesville, PA. Many of these letters spoke of the hardships the men were having in finding work and their worries about home life without them. Some letters from grandfather explained why there was no money to send home: one letter suggested that Daisy sell the family cow.

"Grandma; Can you tell me some of your greatest joys and your deepest sorrows?"

There are several letters from Bob and Jack, the oldest of Daisy's boys. These were obviously very precious keepsakes and her children and husband were the stars in her crown, her greatest joy. She kept an undated piece of paper that was filled with childish pencil scribbles, lines and waves which were obviously very precious to her.

On 9 February 1910 Richard Stoughton Caughey died from typhoid fever. His grandfather, John Caughey wrote that,

> *"he was an angel of a boy...I can see his little face...God will keep him safe."*

Little Richard is buried in the Sewickley Cemetery in the family plot in an unmarked grave. (Section F Lot 92 Grave #3) The only visible reminder of Richard is in the letters and cards of condolences sent to Mrs. J. S. Caughey, Green Street, Sewickley, Pa. Also, in The Treasure Box there is a small envelop labeled, *Master Richard's Tooth.* Daisy and John lost their only daughter, Josephine Lee, at the age of six months on 18 January 1911. Josephine is buried in the unmarked grave #4 of the family plot in Sewickley Cemetery. The death of these two little ones saddened Daisy's heart for the rest of her days.

Daisy's Treasure Box was filled with memories that she cherished. No letters were saved in this particular box once the family was reunited in 1913. From the letters of reference and from reading each letter and scrap of paper, along with my personal knowledge, anyone who met Daisy Maude McCormick Caughey loved her. She was deeply religious and dedicated to her family and to her nursing profession. She was humble, generous and cheerful, a devoted wife and mother and not one to complain about life's sorrows. John obviously loved her and she him. Daisy's Treasure Box was filled with treasure, but the best treasure was that she was my grandmother.

Daisy with her sons: Jack, Edward, Robert, Dan, and Paul. Circa 1917.

VII

ROBERT MCCORMICK CAUGHEY

1902 - 1929

WORLD WAR I

Robert was the oldest child of John Stevens and Maude McCormick Caughey. He was born 6 July 1902 at home in Old Economy, Beaver County, Pennsylvania.[56] At the age of 7, Robert was living with his parents, John and Maude; his brothers John and Paul; his cousin Fannie E. Caughey; his paternal grandmother, Sara and his maternal aunt, Edna McCormick on Green Street in Sewickley, Allegheny County, Pennsylvania.[57] Robert was not enumerated with his parents for the 1920 census and I have not been able to locate where he was living in 1920.

---

[56] Certificate of Death Commonwealth of Pennsylvania department of Health Bureau of Vital Statistics File #118126 Registration District 02-25-41.

[57] 1910 U.S. Census, Allegheny County, Pennsylvania, population schedule, Sewickley, p. 13B, John S. Caughey; NARA microfilm Roll T624_1297.

Robert married Bertha Shearer, daughter of Charles and Ida Moyer Shearer on 17 October 1927.[58] Together they applied for a marriage license on 26 August 1927. She was a clerk and living at home and he was a salesman. They wed in Loudonville, Richland County, Ohio, home of the bride and then they moved to Glenfield, Allegheny, Pennsylvania, home of the groom. Robert was a radio supplies salesman for Joseph Horne's, a large department store in Pittsburgh.

Their daughter, Bertha was born on 6 July 1928. She died at birth and was buried in the Sewickley Cemetery in Section F, Lot 92, unmarked grave # 6. The Sewickley Cemetery Interment Records show that John S. and his brother, S.N. Caughey were owners of the lot. This is the only known record of infant Bertha.[59] Also in Section F, Lot 92, unmarked grave #3 in Richard Stoughton Caughey, age 4, son of John S. and Maude and in unmarked grave #4, their only daughter, Josephine Lee Caughey, 6 months old. What a precious little plot of ground these unmarked graves hold, surrounded by mature oaks, maples and beautiful stone walls.

Robert died very young on 8 December 1929.[60] His obituary from the Ashland Times-Gazette reads: "Robert Caughey died Saturday evening at his home at

---

[58] Family Search, "Pennsylvania Marriages 1885-1950," database (accessed 26 Oct 2012) Robert McCormick Caughey and Bertha Shearer, FHL# 388,750.
[59] Sewickley Cemetery , Sewickley, Allegheny, PA, Interment Records, p. 33.
[60] Death Notice Ashland Times-Gazette Wed. Dec. 11,1929 p. 12 column 5 "Loudonville News" Robert Caughey.

Sewickley, Pa. following pneumonia. Funeral services were held in the above city. Tuesday at 2p.m. Mrs. Caughey was formerly Bertha Shearer of Loudonville."

How do we know Robert was a veteran? The only record that I have found stating that Robert McCormick Caughey was a World War I veteran is from a project the Pennsylvania Historical and Museum Commission created: The Pennsylvania Veterans Burial cards, 1929-1990. Notes from his card are: Robert's birth: 1902 and death: 8 Dec 1929. Veteran: World War Cemetery: Sewickley, Pa Sec 7 Lot 96 grave 7[61]

It is well known that many men were exposed to mustard gas during WWI as well as being exposed to deplorable conditions in the trenches across Europe. Was Robert exposed to mustard gas which weakened his lungs and he was susceptible to pneumonia? I don't know. Was Robert in the trenches in Europe. I don't know. All we can say for sure is that Robert was a World War I veteran and we thank him for his service and his sacrifice. His mother mourned his death the rest of her days [62]and so did his wife. Bertha never remarried and she lived with her mother-in-law, Maude once John died. She returned to school and became a

---

[61] Pennsylvania Veterans Burial Cards, 1929-1990; Archive Collection Number: Series 1-2; Folder Number 80.

[62] Private collection of Diaries from 1952-1963. On July 6, of each diary entry, Robert's mother, Daisy Maude, recalls his birth and death. In the 1955 diary, held in private by Lynne C. Holden, granddaughter, Robert's mother wrote: "and with his Maker twenty five years and still the agony of that sad time is very poignant. There are happy memories of his dear sweet life and these times I love to remember. His happy whistle as he came home from school."

nurse. At the tender age of 23 she had lost her only child and at the age of 24 she was a widow.

Robert takes his place in history as a veteran of World War I, the "war to end all wars." Robert's brothers, John, Paul and Edward would be part of the "Greatest Generation," a term coined by Tom Brokaw. This generation grew up during the Great Depression of 1930 and went on to fight in World War II. Neither of these wars was a 'war to end all wars'-nor the war to make the world safe. Yet, each veteran in his or her own way stepped forward to serve and sacrificed for country and family.

Sewickley Cemetery
Broad and Hopkins Street
Sewickley, PA 15143

VIII

WHAT I REMEMBER OF WWII

DAVID G. CAUGHEY

The first thought I remember about World War II-Mother made white bib overalls for brother, Bobby and me. She sewed big red V's, for victory onto the fronts. We carried a shovel and a hoe and stood on stage reciting:

> *We are the Victory Garden twins.*
> *We're ready, yes ready for work,*
> *We're not very big but our garden we'll dig*
> *And you'll find that we never will shirk!*

I was 7 and in the 2nd grade when Dad was drafted. He would soon turn 36 and was thus among the oldest of draftees. He could have applied for a deferment because of his age, his job, and he had a young family, but he said, "If they need me, I will go" and besides his company, Hazel-Atlas Glass, didn't make anything he thought essential-"just cold cream jars for the army."

Dad reported to duty Jan. 7, 1944 and our lives changed. It was a bleak winter. Mother took in a boarder, but she was afraid of him. We had chickens. The feed sacks were too heavy to lift so they were stored in the basement. Rats took up residence there and we would hear them in the night dragging things around. The hard work, coal furnace, isolation, a 7 year old and 2 year old made it rough on our city-raised mother.

Mother persevered. When summer finally came, with school out, we boarded a Pullman sleeper for York Beach, Maine where Dad had rented a cottage. He was stationed at the US Naval Hospital in Portsmouth, NH and could spend leave and week-ends with us. After three weeks on the beach and flounder fishing we were back home.

Mother had divided our large garden into three "Victory Gardens." We kept one from which we canned beans, corn, beets, and tomatoes. In Sept. I started the 3rd grade. We students saved our pennies to buy savings stamps, collected grease, scrap metal, and milkweed pods for stuffing life jackets. We thought a lot about the evil Hitler and what we wanted to do to him.

Winter came and by this time Dad was on his way to Guam where he would spend the last 11 months of the war at Fleet Hospital 115. We stayed home until Christmas 1944 but Mother had had enough! We moved from Gabby to Edgeworth to live with her parents David and Anna Grattan.

To me it seemed like a miracle! My grandfather, David Grattan, the police chief, became my substitute father. The school was huge with an indoor tiled bathroom. The teacher was pretty. She smiled a lot and didn't hit. The streets had sidewalks and street lights. Everyone wanted me to succeed, it seemed, in this new place, so with much help and effort I learned to multiply. Dad sent presents from Guam: a coconut made into a bank, and lots of letters.

The war was finally over and I was in the 4th grade. Mr. Ellenberger, a neighbor, and I celebrated setting off firecrackers which he had saved to mark the end of the war. Dad was discharged Dec 12, 1945.

IX

PAUL HARPER CAUGHEY
PHARMACIST'S MATE SECOND CLASS

Service Number 923-46-04

He served active duty: Jan 7, 1944-Dec 12, 1945, (1 year, 11 months, 12 days), Bainbridge, MD basic training, USN Hospital, Portsmouth, NH, US Fleet Hospital #115, Guam.

Paul Harper Caughey

X

SAMUEL N. CAUGHEY, JR.

MAY 11, 1911 - FEBRUARY 14, 1969

WW II

We always called him, "Uncle Sam" but in truth he was our first cousin once removed. His father went by the name of Neal. "Uncle Sam" was a bachelor who lived in Sewickley, PA when I was growing up in the 1950s. I remember Sam as a kind, quiet, unassuming man, who was devoted to my grandmother, Daisy. Sam wore a hearing aid. I do not know if his loss of hearing was war related. But, I do remember the long chord attached to the ear piece and the little box he carried in his shirt pocket. To a child that was the most remarkable thing about "Uncle Sam." Sam died at the Sewickley Hospital on 14 February 1969.

Sam joined the Army on 17 December 1942. He was mustered out as a Tech4 on 29 Dec 1945. When he was separated from the Army he had been assigned to the Motor Pool Department and School Troup as a baker, preparing breads, rolls, cookies, pies, cakes and other pastries. From 27 April 1943 through 2 Dec 1945 Sam was in Foreign Service which included Greenland. [63] He was entitled to wear the Good Conduct Medal, World War ll Victory Medal and European African Middle Eastern Campaign Medal.[64]

Prior to entering the Army, Sam was a Welder's Helper at Bethlehem Steel Company, Leetsdale, PA. At the time of his death he was a punch operator.[65] His avocation was the Boy Scouts of the USA. He was Assistant Scoutmaster of Troop 641, member of the Order of the Arrow, Boy Scouts of America. He had also been active in Troop 242 and the Cub Scout program in the Sewickley area.[66]

Sam, along with his parents, Samuel Neal and Laura Caughey, are buried in the Middletown Cemetery, Middletown, PA. A WWll marker is at his grave site: Lot 74 Dn (new) Grave 3-C. Sam served his country with honor during the war. President Truman sent him a letter of thanks from a "grateful Nation. As one of the Nation's finest, you undertook the most severe task one can be called upon to perform. Because you demonstrated the fortitude, resourcefulness and calm

---

[63] *Pennsylvania Veteran Compensation Application Files, WWII, 1950-1959,* Ancestry.com. Caughey, Samuel N.

[64] *Enlisted Record and Report of Separation*. U.S. Government Pub. January 28, 1946, Vol. 73, p. 387. (Privately held)
[65] Commonwealth of Pennsylvania Department of Health Vital Statistic Local Registrar's Certification of Death. No. 17292, Registered No. 75. Samuel N. Caughey. (Privately held)
[66] Obituary Sewickley Herald , Sewickley, PA unknown date. "Samuel N. Caughey" On Friday, February 14, 1969, Samuel N. Caughey of 524 Locust Place, Sewickley.

judgment necessary to carry out that task, we now look to you for leadership and example in further exalting our country in peace."

Samuel N. Caughey, Jr.

Middletown Cemetery, Middletown, PA

XI

JOHN SHIPLETT "JACK" CAUGHEY

BORN FEBRUARY 13, 1924

HE WAS MY DAD

JANET CAUGHEY KESSLER

It is Christmas, 2014, and my father has been gone for 6 years now. I think about him every day, without fail.

My father graduated from high school in 1942. He was 18 years old. Now, think about when you were 18 years old. Chances are you are going to go to college in a couple of months, and you're excited about that. If you're a guy, your testosterone is going crazy and you've got girlfriends galore. I know my dad had a girlfriend with the unfortunate name of Helma Butt (yes, really) and another girlfriend named Alice Ann. He didn't know my mom yet. He was young and in his prime. However, the world was at war; had been for only 6 months when the Japanese bombed Pearl Harbor on December 7, 1941. The thought of this war was probably never far from his mind. He was precisely the type and age of person that our country was looking for. Dad was probably resigned to the fact that he SHOULD go to fight for his country, but he was also feeling honor bound to do it. He was that kind of guy. When something needed to be done, he always had the attitude of "Let's do it." In the immortal words of Larry the Cable Guy, Dad's mantra was always, "Git 'er done!"

So 8 months after he graduated high school, he enlisted in the Army, on February 22, 1943. He was 19 years and 9 days old. He was a kid! That was a huge decision to make, to devote his next few years to service of his country instead of joining a fraternity or trying out for the football team at Ohio University. It was the right thing to do, and he did it.

Unfortunately, his life in the Army is a big blank space to me, his daughter. I was born in 1951; the war was over. Dad had been home for 6 years, was married, and was already a father to a son, born in March of 1948. His life continued in Zanesville, Ohio, and it was many years before I was even cognizant that a war had taken place just in the last decade. I rarely if ever asked my dad about his war service, and he never talked about it. Men of his generation, I have learned, were very stoic and did not talk about their war-time adventures, if you will. I know he served his basic training at the Great Lakes camp, which I believe is in the vicinity of Chicago. I know that he served in the Philippines. I know that he contracted a medical condition commonly known at the time as "jungle rot" and spent quite a lot of time at a hospital in Hawaii.

My dad wrote many letters to his mother, my grandmother, and I remember reading one of them where he casually referred to "shooting a couple Japs." I remember thinking this did not sound like my dad, who never ever disparaged a race of people with insulting nicknames. (Even when, like the Japanese of the WWII era, they may have deserved it.) Those letters were somehow destroyed. My dad was not a big letter writer, so the fact that he did write to Grandma so often shows that he had things to get off his chest. I just wish I knew what he had gone through. My dad was such a strong man, mentally, but it must have been excruciating for him to actually shoot another person. But then again, in war, maybe it's easy. I don't know. Maybe he put that into a little compartment in his brain so he wouldn't have to think about it.

He was wounded in action during the invasion of Leyte Island on October 20, 1944. I know this because of a newspaper article in the Zanesville Signal my Cousin Lynne unearthed. What I know about the invasion of Leyte is what I found out just now on Wikipedia. Dad did not tell us about it. Dad bore a scar on the top of his head, like a little dent. I did ask him about that, and he said he was sitting in a Jeep, took off his hat to scratch his head, and it felt like someone had whacked him with a frying pan. Next thing he knew, there was blood running down his face, and he thought, "Wow, what just happened to me?" He was 20 years old. If the bullet had been ONE INCH lower, Dad would have been another casualty of World War II. He would not have met Mom. My brother would not be here. I would not be here. He received the Purple Heart for being wounded in service. He was really proud of that medal. When he showed it to me, I was not impressed. Who wants a PURPLE medal? I did not get it at all. He also received two Bronze Stars in the course of his service. I do not know what happened to them.

Jack in Guam.

Dad never seemed to have any ill effects from having served in the military. There was no "post traumatic stress disorder" diagnosis back then, but it most assuredly existed. I don't remember my dad ever having problems of any sort. He was a happy man, a funny man, a decent and caring man, who wanted nothing more than what he had: a nice house, a wife, and two children who ADORED him. Heck, all the kids in the neighborhood adored him. When Dad came home from working at Hazel Atlas, later Continental Can, later Brockway Glass, in Zanesville, it was an EVENT. Dad got up at 3:00 in the morning 5 days a week, so that he could put in over-time at the glass plant. He got off at 3:00 in the afternoon. That's a 12-hour work-day, a 60-hour work week. And yet, when he got home, he was always ready to play a game of whiffle-ball, or croquet, or badminton with us kids in the back yard. I think about that, and if I'd put in that hard day in a HOT glass plant, I'd have been more inclined to tell us kids, "Hey, leave me alone! Honey, get me a beer!" Not Dad.

So, knowing my Dad as I did, I can tell you for certain what kind of a soldier he was. He did what he was told. He did not EVER complain. He always knew what he was doing was for the greater good. He was proud. He was a good companion to his fellow soldiers. He lightened the mood every chance he got. He was a "hoot". He did not resent the time he lost serving in the war or languishing at the hospital in Hawaii. He "got 'er done!" and then he came home and had a wonderful life.

I have a picture on my wall of my dad, my young dad who still had hair, wearing some baggy clothes and standing next to his beloved Uncle Ed, who was more his contemporary in age. They are in Guam, according to my Cousin Lynne, Ed's daughter who sent me the picture. He is somewhere between 19 and 21 years old. He is smiling just like he is in his senior picture in the Lash High School yearbook. He doesn't have a care in the world, and he's thrilled to be with his Uncle Ed. He is HAPPY.

That was my dad, truly an extraordinary man who was happiest when he was with his family, his uncles, Dan, Paul, and Ed, his dad, Jack Sr., his wife Jean, and us kids. He was on this earth for 84 years, and he left to be with his uncles and his dad and mom on April 24, 2008. He was happy on Earth, and he is happy in Heaven.

Ed and Jack in Guam.

XII

"JOIN THE NAVY
AND SEE THE WORLD"

EDWARD LINDSEY CAUGHEY

NOVEMBER 1, 1916 - MAY 5, 2005

Our Dad had not been a world traveler prior to his enlistment in the United States Navy in 1943. He was born in Sewickley, Pennsylvania and he attended the Sewickley High School, graduating in June 1935. When he was four years old his parents, John Stevens and Daisy McCormick Caughey moved to Zanesville, Ohio where their oldest son, John St. Clair Caughey lived. But within five years they returned to Glenfield, Pennsylvania, where he attended elementary school and when it was time for Sewickley high school, Glenfield was close enough for Ed to walk. Following graduation he went to Penn State in State College, PA where he majored in Metallurgy and graduated with a B.Sc. degree in 1939. During the summers he worked for his father who had a small restaurant/creamery on Broad Street, Sewickley. He was not what one would call a seasoned traveler: Sewickley, Glenfield, State College and as far west as Zanesville, Ohio.

Dad met Helen Mellott at a college Christmas party. He had a car which made him quite popular with the girls and Helen liked the car. Ed "fell" for Helen and the car had been an asset. And so the story unfolded that they fell in love, got engaged and married on 11 June 1941 at the Presbyterian Church in Ambridge, PA. Helen's parents, Dr. Albert N. and Anna Clark Mellott, did not think Edward was just right for their daughter because he came from a different social background and they had other hopes and dreams for their oldest daughter. Perhaps that is why Ed worked hard all his life to show his in-laws that he was perfectly capable of taking care of Helen in the "style to which she was accustomed."

The young couple moved to Youngstown, Ohio where Ed worked for the Republic Steel Company as a metallurgist, responsible for the timing of when the molten steel was ready to be poured. They had an apartment at 1660 East Midlothian Boulevard, Youngstown, Mohoning County, Ohio.

Ed and Helen had enjoyed six months as newlyweds and Helen was 2 months pregnant when Pearl Harbor was bombed by the Japanese on 7 December 1941. Now the call for steel was even more important. All the steel companies in Ohio and western Pennsylvania were on high production. One of the dichotomies of war amidst great sacrifice and suffering is that much money can be made in industries such as steel and the manufacturing of ammunitions and other goods and services associated with related war activities. Republican Steel in Youngstown, Ohio was no exception. Our Dad had job security. But the draft board was calling up young men at a fast pace. At some point our Dad decided within himself that he would rather chose the branch of service than be drafted, so in early March 1943, Dad enlisted in the Navy and was to report for Officer Training School at Quonset Point, Rhode Island in April 1943. His wife was, in her words, "hysterical" when he came home to tell her he had enlisted. She was far from home and now with a small child. At some point, Helen called her father and asked to come back to Ambridge for the duration of the war as long as her husband would be away from home. Her father said "No" because, "A small child would be a disruption to his medical practice." Our maternal grandfather worked as one of the doctors for the American Bridge Company and he also had a medical practice on the main floor of their home at 600 Maplewood Avenue, Ambridge, PA. I, Lynne, was that small child, a toddler and I am sure I would have been a disruption. But, my mother's life was suddenly disrupted too and the country was at war. I know that mother carried that rejection for the rest of her life.

Dad and mother left Ohio and had time to find an apartment for mother and Lynne in Ben Avon, PA, just up the Ohio River from Ambridge. I have several photos of mother and me with the neighbors from our "walk-up" apartment, the apartment that my brother, Robert Edward, known as Ted, joined us on 16 June 1944.

Dad "graduated" from Officers Training, entering active service on 27 April 1943 with the rank of

U.S.S. Kasaan Bay (CVE 69). The Kasaan Bay received one battle star for World War II service.

Ensign. He would be separated from Active service on 2 December 1945 in Philadelphia, PA as a Lieutenant (junior grade). Following the end of the war, Ed remained active in the Naval Reserves and when he finally retired from the Reserves he did so with the rank of Lieutenant Commander.

After Ed's training in Rhode Island he reported to San Francisco in December 1943 and there he joined the crew as the Catapult Officer and Junior Division Officer on the escort carrier U.S.S. *Kasaan Bay (CVE 69)*. He served in that capacity until Oct 1945.

My mother and I accompanied Dad to San Francisco. We went by train, with sleeping cars. Mother loved to tell the story that I was quite the hit with the many service men traveling off to war and unknown parts of the world when I was just 17 months old. My brother, Ted, likes to say his middle name should be "Pullman." It would have been a long sad train ride back across country for our mother once we bid farewell to a husband and father; mother facing the unknown and having to live in a walk up apartment with a small child, alone, soon to find she was pregnant again. The men and women who deserve our thanks for their service always leave behind family: parents, lovers, companions, children and friends who also sacrifice much for the sake of their country. Our Mother, like countless other young wives, somehow coped for the duration of the war.

For a man who had had very little travel experiences, that was about to change. "Join the Navy and See the World," is not just a slogan, for our Dad it became a reality. On 8 January 1944 the *Kasaan Bay* departed San Francisco with a cargo of planes and sailed for Pearl Harbor. From Pearl Harbor the ship returned to San Diego and then departed for refurbishing at Norfolk, VA. From the shores of Virginia the ship and crew would patrol along the East Coast. On 28 May 1944 she departed New York with a cargo of planes for Casablanca, Morocco. I wonder if our parents ever had a chance to see Humphrey Bogart and Ingrid Bergman in the Academy Award winning movie, *Casablanca,* before he shipped out to sea? On the return to New York from Africa, the crew had rescued 342 survivors of the U.S.S. *Block Island (CVE 21)*. The *Block Island* had been torpedoed on May 29th, the only U.S. military ship lost in the Atlantic Theater during World War II. The *Kassan Bay* was close enough to hear the distress calls and arrived to rescue the crew members and take them back to New York. (As an interesting note, sixty five years later I served The Harbor Church on Block Island, the very place for which CVE 21 was named.)

"Kassie," as the escort carrier was called by the crew, departed Quonset Point, RI, on June 30th and arrived at Oran, Algeria July 10th. Throughout July of 1944 she engaged in patrol and flight operations in the Mediterranean and rehearsed for the assault on Southern France and the area of the French Riviera. Planes from the carrier bombed and strafed German positions, destroying hundreds of enemy vehicles and tanks and downing two enemy aircraft over the bench. These were tense and busy days. The *Kasaan Bay* headed into the wind from dawn to dusk, launching, and landing over 450 planes. Not a single plane or pilot was seriously injured aboard the Kasaan Bay. As Catapult Officer our Dad's working day was often 24 hours. Dad received a letter of commendation for his skills and attention to details during this battle in Southern French waters. On August 20th, pilot, Lieutenant Commander Harry Brinkley Bass, was killed while on a strafing mission near Saint-Bonnet-le-Froid, France. He was the ships' sole casualty during action. Fifty two years later, our Dad and his granddaughter, Debra Brooker Hurteau, would return to Southern France and dedicate a memorial to LCDR Brinkley Bass. On 30 August 1944 the carrier left Algeria and arrived at Norfolk 12 days later.

Following her Mediterranean tour of duty, the carrier was assigned to the Pacific Fleet, sailing to Pearl Harbor, Guam, and Ulithi of the Caroline Islands. She carried planes and various replacements for other ships of the Fast Carrier Task Force. The *Kasaan Bay* patrolled the waters and shipping lanes between the Marshall and Mariana Islands protecting the fleet's supply line during the final assault on Japan's defenses. Dad had now served in the Atlantic and the Pacific Theaters and had crossed the International Date Line several times. He had become a seasoned sailor, a world traveler, one who had sailed the Mediterranean as well.

When hostilities ended on 14 August 1945, the *Kasaan Bay* returned to Guam where she was assigned "Magic- Carpet" duty. In Guam, Ed had a reunion with his nephew, John "Jack" Shiplett Caughey, one of those remarkable coincidences' of the war that our Dad liked to talk about. John had his own "magic carpet" trip back to the states.

The carrier departed Saipan on 13 September 1945 with her first group of returning veterans arriving in San Diego. For the next three months she made three cruises to Hawaii and the Philippines to transport homeward bound troops to the United States.

The escort carrier returned to the East Coast arriving in Boston on 22 February 1945. It was a grand reunion for Ed and Helen. In nine months, Ed would officially be separated from the Navy in time for Christmas, the very best Christmas ever![67]

---

[67] Dictionary of American Fighting Ships, Vol. III, 1968, Navy Department. Office of the Chief of Naval Operations, Naval History Division, Washington D.C.

http://www.ibiblio.org/hyper-war/USN/ships/dafs/CVE/cve69.html

Letter of Commendation as it appeared inThe HERALD, Sewickley, Pa., Thursday, May 17, 1945. Vol. 42 No 20 pg 1.

Lt (jg) Edward L. Caughey, son of Mr. and Mrs. John S. Caughey of Washington, Pa., formerly of Sewickley, has been awarded a commendation by the Commander of the Eighth Fleet and is entitled to wear a commendation ribbon. The special notice was given for his "Outstanding performance of duty while serving as Catapult Officer of a U.S. Navy aircraft carrier during the amphibious invasion of Southern France in August, 1944."

The commendation reads in part, "You exhibited great professional skill and tireless energy in supervising the expeditions and efficient operation of the catapult machinery of the _____. With inspiring leadership and careful attention to detail, you directed the launching of four hundred and fifty aircraft without material or personnel casualties and thus contributed materially to the ability of the planes of the _____ to fulfill completely a strenuous flight schedule despite adverse conditions for normal takeoff, and to render effective air support to the ground forces on the beachheads. I commend you for your exceptional ability, resourcefulness and outstanding devotion to duty, which reflected credit upon yourself and the Naval Service.

H.K. Hewitt

Edward as ensign

Our Remembrances of our Dad's Naval Reserve Days, written collaboratively by his children, Lynne, "Ted," Nancy and Martha.

NANCY CAUGHEY BOWERMASTER

When I think of Dad's Navy Reserve Days I remember he was always in a dress uniform with his hat. He was so handsome. On one occasion I was asleep on the landing and I woke to a fuzzy ball of fur under my arm. She was just a puppy and she had snuggled into my arm pit and had fallen asleep with me. I awoke to this copper colored "Lassie" type dog which I instantly fell in love with. We named her Penny. She was a very special member of our family from that night on.

LYNNE CAUGHEY HOLDEN

I have fond memories of Halloween and our costumes. One year I used a particular "Service Dress White" Navy jacket, that was once brilliant porcelain but then was old, aged and the color of cream. Yet, the buttons were still shiny like the one button I now keep in my jewelry box. The jacket had a stand-up collar. Dad said the jacket was referred to by the men as "chokers." In any case, I was allowed to use the jacket for Halloween in this way: I put two small holes near the pockets of the jacket so that when I put the jacket on top of my head I could see out, but it looked as if I had no head. I covered the top of my hair with a red scarf so that "choker collar" was resting on a bloody stump. Under my arm I carried my head: a football wearing one of those ugly, creepy, scary rubber masks. I was the "Headless Horseman." I am sure the Navy would never have approved the use of the uniform. But the kids I hung around with thought it was a great idea and that year I think I even got lots of candy!

MARTHA ANNE CAUGHEY

When I was asked to reiterate my memories of my father's reserve service to the Navy my answer was I have no memories. What I do remember was thinking how handsome my father was in his uniformed pictures that hung somewhere in the house. I knew he was in a war that was supposed to be the "war to end all wars." I was very confused about what the war was all about since I was raised to go to church and learn the Ten Commandments. "Thou Shall Not Kill" made me wonder why and how could anyone fight a war. How could anyone hate a person for being a different color or loving another person even if they were the same sex, or what you want to put in one's pipe to smoke? Vietnam came along when I was at the age of 15. I still had the same questions. It wasn't until 9/11 that I decided that war was a necessary evil and Dad had fought to keep the USA a free country. Thank you, Dad. However, we still have a long way to go to truly be the "Land of the Free and the Home of the Brave."

ROBERT "TED" EDWARD CAUGHEY

I watched my dad stand at attention when I was about 13 years old. We were at the naval reserve base in Akron, Ohio. He was showing me all around the base and I was very impressed that everyone had to salute him. Then my dad saluted a guy and I asked dad why he had to salute. Dad said, "Because he has more scrambled eggs on his visor than I have." Later, he got permission to board the admiral's airplane. It was a twin engine Convair. I was sitting in the left seat in the cockpit admiring all the gauges, buttons and switches when a sailor with SP on his arm came running up into the airplane yelling, "who gave that kid permission to be on this airplane?" My father said, "I did." Then the sailor snapped a smart salute to my father and said, "Yes, sir." I thought to myself, 'wow, my father must own this navy.'

Another time, when dad came home from his active 2 week cruise, I was in bed and I heard his voice on the front porch. He was sitting with my mom drinking a cup of coffee. The cup was the cup he carried all through the war. I was so surprised to see him that I jumped on to his lap, and he dropped the coffee cup which shattered all over the floor. He was upset, but he didn't yell at me.

I remember watching him clean the gold braids on the sleeves of his uniform with a little brush, and then shine his shoes until you could see your face in them. These are some of my memories of my dad while serving in the US Navy.

Edward L. Caughey Memorial Service July 24, 2005

Words spoken by David G. Caughey

Of the five Caughey brothers, Ed and my Dad, Paul, were the most alike. Although nine years apart in age, they were best friends from the beginning and remained so for the next eighty-plus years.

Ten year old Ed carried a hot lunch every working day to Paul at his summer job at the Glenfield Box Plant. Ed made huge onion sandwiches and then crawled into bed they shared when Paul was home from college. They swam across the river and got up close to Ohio River steamboats in their canoe. Eventually Ed followed Paul to Penn State. I know all the Caughey brothers didn't honor their father and mother all the time as they were taught but Paul and Ed were different-they were model kids who made their parent's job easy.

In 1995 my mother, Alice, died. Helen was already gone. My family began the tradition of spending a week together in the West Virginia Mountains. Paul said, "Eddie has to come!"- and he did-for the next five or so years. These were his last really good years. He could hike the trails, swim, climb Seneca Rocks, play golf, tease the children and adults, and find his way to bed with a flashlight after late night card games.

In the fall of 1998 my dad was declining. He had a very bad night followed by an early morning trip to the doctor who said, "I'm putting you in the hospital right now." Dad said, "I can't go. My brother is coming for lunch on his yearly trip to Florida." We had a nice visit at lunch and only then did Dad go to the hospital. He didn't come home again.

February 2, Ground Hog Day, Dad's birthday came and the telephone rang. It was Ed. He said, "I always call Paul today and now I don't know who to call, so I called you."

He was a great brother, a great uncle and a great friend.

Edward in Guam.

XIII

THE CAUGHEY
CANADIAN CONNECTION!
BY
DEBRA BROOKER HURTEAU

Proverbs 17:6 "Grandchildren are the crown of the aged, and the Glory of children is their fathers."

This was my grandfather, Ed Caughey. He loved and cared for all his grandchildren and his children all admired him greatly. I was so privileged to visit a beautiful part of the world with him in 1996 in Southern France.

However, before I tell you about our wonderful trip, I must explain why he asked me to accompany him. In 1990, I married Claude Hurteau, a handsome French Canadian, whom I met in Bible College in Baltimore, Maryland. After our first year of marriage, and much to my families despair, we moved to Montreal, Canada, where my prince charming was from. I, being a true American, of course, spoke no other language than English. I quickly realized the importance of learning French in order to survive in "La Belle Province," where the Quebecois are very proud of their French heritage and their language. I picked up the Quebec French dialect quickly and within 2 years could read and write, as well as speak fluently in this romantic tongue.

On May 22, 1995, three days before my 27th birthday, my grandmother, Helen Caughey, suddenly passed away. We were all shaken by her passing, especially her husband of 50+ years. In March, 1996 my grandfather was invited to a memorial service to be held in France, to commemorate a pilot who had served onboard the transport carrier "*Kasaan Bay*". This Navy pilot died during the invasion of Southern France. My Grandfather was a lieutenant and a catapult officer on the "*Kassan Bay*." Just a little side note here: I had no idea what a Catapult Officer was. During our trip, I asked my grandfather what he actually did in the Navy. He, being the engineer that he was, explained it to me in such an easy, comprehensible way. He said that he sling shot the planes in the air, and then caught them with a big hook when they landed.

Well during a family discussion about this invitation my grandfather had received to the memorial service, I jokingly mentioned I would go with him, as I spoke French. I'm not sure of the exact details but I know his children were a bit concerned of him traveling alone; in any case, I received a surprising invitation to accompany him.

In October of 1996, we were off to Haute-Loire, Southern France. I met my grandfather in Paris and we flew together to Lyon, France. There we were greeted by a very passionate Frenchman, Marcel Ertel and his daughter Anne-Marie. Marcel was a historian, who after having served as an air controller in Lyon-Bron and Satoias, France decided to dedicate his time to the lost and forgotten pilots of WWII. He had done much research and had organized the memorial for LCDR Harry Brinkley Bass, the naval pilot that gave his life for their freedom. We, along with many members of Officer Bass's family, and shipmates from the "*Kasaan Bay*" were chauffeured in a French army bus as we participated in the memorial service and dedication. We enjoyed visiting the French country side. Marcel had organized a wonderful visit for us, with the main event being the dedication of the memorial at Les Vilettes near Monistrol for LCDR Harry Brinkley Bass, who gave his life on August 20th, 1944. He had crashed while on a strafing mission in Haute-Loire in the Vallées des Moulins, near Saint Bonnet, Le Froid.

I still feel very privileged to have had the opportunity to spend time with my grandfather and his shipmates. As I am fluent in French and English, I quickly became the translator for M. Ertel, who spoke very little English, as he shared his beautiful country with us. He was an exceptional tour guide, but I think the most moving event was visiting where he believed the crash site took place. Bass's family had, for a long time, believed his crash site to have been near Grenoble, but through Ertel's research, he was able to discover the actual site of this Lieutenant Commander. It was so touching for us to witness the emotions of his family members present as they visited the hillside above a quaint little French farm where their brother had lost his life for freedom.

My Grandfather was always very proud of his years of service with the US Navy, and after spending time with him on this trip, and getting to know a bit more about his time in the Navy and meeting his fellow officers, I too am very proud of my grandfather and the generation of men and women who gave their lives for our freedom.

US COMMÉMORATION

du 5 au 10 Octobre 1996
à l'occasion de l'inauguration de la stèle à la mémoire
du LT CMDR Harry BRINKLEY BASS

SQ - VF 74 / 451 ST BOMBER/GROUP
USS KASAAN BAY (CVE-69) / USS BRINKLEY BASS (DD-887)
HMS HUNTER / HMS STALKER

XIV

CHRISTEN GAIL CAUGHEY CIESLAK

ROBERT P. CAUGHEY

Birth date: Jan 5, 1969

Chris' mother (Lois) handed her an application for an ROTC scholarships and said "Just fill it out. What's the big deal?" Chris and her Dad (Bob) toured colleges and settled on Bucknell or Penn State. Since Bucknell would have been too costly for her parents if she decided to drop the ROTC scholarship, Chris took her scholarship to Penn State and graduated in 1991 in Civil Engineering.

The world was at peace in 1991 and the Army did not need more officers so Chris' obligation was met by joining the Army Reserves.

Chris continued in the Reserves while starting her career as a Civil Engineer, getting married, and having her first child (Cara-May 2001). Following the birth of her second child (John-March 2003) she was deployed to the Iraq war in November of 2003 and served in Kuwait as engineering support for the effort in Iraq.

Chris returned home to Ben Avon and started her own engineering company (Chronicle Consulting). She continued to serve in the Reserves and rose to position of Lieutenant Colonel.

In April of 2011, Chris was again deployed but this time to Afghanistan (Kabul) where she served as engineering support for the troop draw-down effort. During her deployment, Chris' mother (Lois) died suddenly (January 2012). Chris returned home for the services and then returned to finish her term.

Christen Gail Caughey Cieslak

After Chris returned from Afghanistan, she closed her company and took a position with Oxford Development in Pittsburgh. She had some difficulty adjusting to civilian life as well as coping with the loss of her mother. She was eventually recruited by Icon Venue Group, which specializes in major sports stadiums and arenas and is based in Colorado. She is currently working on and travelling to San Antonio, Texas on the NBA Spurs arena project.

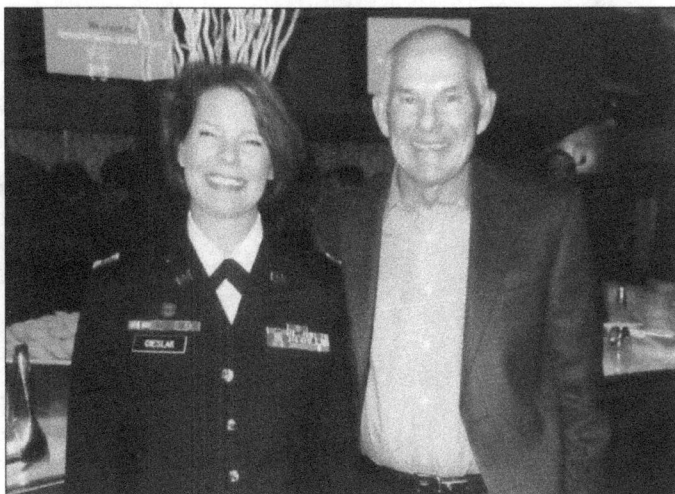

Christen Gail Caughey Cieslak with her dad, Robert Caughey

Chris continues to serve in the Army Reserves as a Lieutenant-Colonel and will probably retire from service in a year or so.

From: Christen:

11 September 2013

This one is from my supervisor, Major General Bryan Watson presenting me with a Bronze Star medal at the end of my tour in Kabul, Afghanistan in 2012. One of my proudest moments.

Here are some links and excerpts to articles about Chris and her deployments:

http://shriverreport.org/wife-mother-soldier-chris-cieslak/

THE SHRIVER REPORT
POWERED BY INFORMATION

Special Edition
Wife, Mother, Soldier

Lt. Col. Chris Cieslak is an Active Drilling Reservist (serving in Troop Program Unit status) and has more than 22 years of services in the Army Reserves. She was commissioned in 1991, has served two terms of deployment (one 6 month deployment to Kuwait, and a one year deployment in Afghanistan), and is a wife and mother of two. She is also a Civil Engineer and, as she puts it, over the course of her "entire professional and adult life, I have been the minority gender." She shares her experience as a woman in the military and explains how she manages being a soldier and a mother, as well as describing her struggles with returning to the realities of civilian life.

TSR: When you enrolled in ROTC (Reserve Officer Training Corp) , did you ever foresee being a Mom and an active service member?

I enrolled in ROTC to appease my mother's request that I apply for a scholarship. When I got the scholarship, she had second thoughts, but I figured I ought to at least give it a try. My dad's advice has always been to "keep doors open,, so accepting the scholarship and enrolling in ROTC as a freshman was in keeping with that advice. I did not think much beyond that, and was ambivalent about being a mother in the future.

TSR: How have you resolved the pull between the roles of being in the military and being in a parent?

My maternal instinct is not particularly strong, and I have a husband with a much stronger maternal instinct than mine! Having a partner who is more engaged that I ever wanted to be in the day-to-day aspects of raising children has made it much easier to be in the military. We have taken the approach that we each specialize in our respective roles, so I can go off and do this work without (too much) guilt.

TSR: When you returned to civilian life, did you and your husband maintain the roles that exist while you were in Afghanistan – where he is the primary caregiver?

Yes, we started that after my first deployment in 2004. When I returned, I decided to go into business for myself and that necessitated that we continue the same division of responsibility. Since 2004, I have mostly forgotten how to cook, do crafts, and pay the bills.

From The Shriver Report, November 11, 2013

http://www.post-gazette.com/stories/life/life-style/soldiers-story-a-year-in-afghanistan-changes-lt-col-chris-cieslak-and-her-family-633595/

Pittsburgh Post-Gazette
post-gazette.com
April 29, 2012 12:45 PM

Soldier's Story: A year in Afghanistan changes Lt. Col Chris Cieslak, and her family

Back together: in Ben Avon Jeff and Chris Cieslak with children Johnny and Cara and Simon the dog.

By Gretchen McKay Pittsburgh Post-Gazette

This is the last in a series on Lt. Col. Chris Cieslak's deployment to Afghanistan:

A bunch of red, white and blue balloons danced at the front door when Lt. Col. Chris Cieslak came home earlier this month after a year in Afghanistan. But the rest of her homecoming didn't exactly go as expected.

The Ben Avon Army reservist ended up returning to the United States the same week her husband, Jeff, had planned a spring break getaway for the kids to a water park in Ohio. So instead of one of those teary reunions at the airport, she was picked up by a friend and dropped off at a house that was as silent as it was empty.

Missing that storybook ending would drive more than a few soldiers crazy. Col. Cieslak isn't one of them. Chalk it up to an engineer's way of thinking, but to her, the fact her family waited until the next day to rush home so they could finish their vacation was an example of them continuing to live life to the fullest while she completed her service.

"At first, I was upset they wouldn't be there to greet me," she acknowledged earlier this month, just two weeks back into civilian life. "Then I thought, 'Wait a sec ... They didn't sit on the sidelines when I was in Afghanistan and watch life pass by.'"

From The Pittsburgh Post Gazette, April 29, 2012

http://www.post-gazette.com/stories/business/news/women-finding-tough-life-after-war-691221/

Pittsburgh Post-Gazette
post-gazette.com

June 11, 2013 4:30 AM

Symposium in Pittsburgh focusing on female veterans

Lt. Col. Chris Cieslak -- Ben Avon resident is a keynote speaker at the symposium

By Joyce Gannon Pittsburgh Post-Gazette

Chris Cieslak returned to Pittsburgh in April 2012 after a year's duty as a U.S. Army Reserves officer in Kabul, Afghanistan, and was showered with praise by family, friends and professional colleagues.

But by that June, the project director for Oxford Development Co. felt as if she had slammed into a brick wall of depression that left her feeling like a fraud.

"People had been putting me on a pedestal ... constantly giving me positive feedback about being brave. I knew I needed help but I didn't know what help I needed."

Fortunately for Ms. Cieslak, who is now a lieutenant colonel with a reserves unit based in Coraopolis, she has a supportive husband; an employer that encouraged her to slow down and mend emotionally; and the resources to seek therapy, medication and yoga classes to help sort out her post-deployment issues.

To help address the issues, the United Way of Allegheny County has coordinated a symposium to be held today, that will include expert speakers and panel discussions about topics specific to female veterans, including housing options, mental health concerns and outreach services. The Eden Hall Foundation is sponsoring the event along with the Veterans Leadership Program.

From The Pittsburgh Post Gazette, June 11, 2013

CLOSING REMARKS

From the descendants of James and Elizabeth Coulter Caughey, men and women have served their country with distinction, honor and courage. Their spouses, companions and children carried on without them, doing their part to be of support to their loved ones and to the particular conflict at hand. There are many other Caughey folk who have served not highlighted in this volume. Miles A Caughey, Jr. and Senior and Daniel Marsh Caughey, Jr. and his son Patrick have all served in the US ARMY; Dan for 22 years and Patrick served seven with two combat tours of duty in Afghanistan and Iraq. Dan met his wife, Helga in Seoul, Korea. Helga was there with the Foreign Service of her native Austria and Dan was there as an Army Captain. Dan retired from the active serve as a Lieutenant Colonel. Richard "Dick" Caughey, son of John S. and Sara Anna (Shiplett) Caughey, was a Korean War veteran of the U.S. Marine Corps and attained the rank of Lt. Col. I am sure there are many other Caughey men and women who should be included in our gratitude for their service.

Scripture tells us to "look to the rock from which you were hewn and the quarry from which you were dug." (Isaiah 51:1)

Lexington and Concord, Bunker Hill, and the deciding battle at Yorktown are the bedrock of this nation's quarry. The Star Spangled Banner was waving at

Fort McHenry in 1812 and, that too, is part of our nation's rock.

Our "Caughey" quarry includes men who heard about the battles at Gettysburg and Shiloh, who guarded the railroad lines from Maryland to Pennsylvania, and who witnessed their country trying to tear itself apart. Even today there is left a guilty land with unresolved tensions over the very issues of which the Civil War was fought. George Washington is the father of our country, the bedrock of our quarry, but it was Abraham Lincoln that held this nation together.

We are cut from the quarry of San Juan Hill, Manila Bay, the Philippines, Hawaii and Guam: places made famous in the Spanish American War. John Hays, Secretary of State under William McKinley said, "It was a splendid little war." Is any war splendid?

The "War to End All Wars" started over one hundred years ago. The U.S. officially joined the war in 1917, but for those who served in our Navy guarding the shipping lanes from U-Boat attacks, they knew great sacrifices lay ahead. Could they foresee the trenches of France, the plague of mustard gas, the great battles of Verdun, Tannerberg and Vimy Ridge?

WWll has etched into the hearts of Americans names like Pearl Harbor, Normandy, Anzio, Midway, Okinawa, Burma and Guadalcanal. My dad always pondered the rationale of Hiroshima and Nagasaki....such great evil in the name of freedom.

And then the soldiers and sailors of my uncles' and father's generation came home, many went to school on the GI bill. They started the baby boom, put a man on the moon and quietly went about their jobs, never asking for, nor expecting, our tributes and thanks.

Meanwhile, war flared again in places far away from our shores: places in Korea and Vietnam, Iraq and Afghanistan. Service men and women fought anew in jungles and deserts, in frigid mountains of North Korea and some went deep under the seas hunting for the "Red October." Our quarry, the rock from which we are hewn, includes men and women willing to serve their country wearing the uniform of a soldier, sailor, marine, or airman. These men and women went to war to protect a way of life and to allow us to live in freedom and peace. They did not seek recognition. Some returned to an angry nation and they were scorned. Some returned to a grateful nation and they were hailed as conquering heroes. And sadly, some returned and have faded into the anonymity of homelessness, joblessness and drug/alcohol addiction. Those of us who have benefitted from the call to service by our veterans must be held responsible to hold all our veterans in gratitude and to work to end the scourge of society's evils that prevents all citizens the rights and responsibilities of life, liberty and the pursuit of happiness. The rock from which we were hewn demands nothing less.

APPENDIX A

Descendants of James and Elizabeth Coulter Caughey

Children of James and Elizabeth Coulter Caughey

-James Caughey b. 11-3-1792, Northern Ireland, d. 4-27-1881, Allegheny City , Allegheny, .PA, bur. 4-28-1881, Union Dale Cemetery, Pittsburgh, Allegheny, PA. Div. One, Lot 13, Range 4, Sec M, Grave 5.

Elizabeth Coulter b. 8-12-1794, Northern Ireland, d. 9-30-1882, Allegheny City, Allegheny, PA, bur. 10-2-1882, Union Dale Cemetery, Pittsburgh, Allegheny, PA Div One, Lot 13, Range 4, Sec M, Grave 4.

> 2-William James Caughey b. 7-11-1817, Pennsylvania, d. 1882, Pennsylvannia

> 2-Mary Caughey b. 10-29-1818, Burgettstown, Washington Co., PA, d. 5-1-1883, Allegheny County, PA

> 2-Clement Paterson Caughey b. 11-3-1820, Burgettstown, Washington Co., PA, d. 1-25-1899, Allegheny County, PA, bur. Highwood Cemetery Section Q 2800 Brighton Rd Pgh, PA

> 2-John Caughey b. 1-6-1823, Burgettstown, Washington Co., PA, d. 11-7-1904, Haysville, Allegheny Co., PA, bur. 11-9-1904, Sewickley Cemetery, Sewickley, Allegheny, PA Sec F Lot 92 Grave 1

> 2-Robert Coulter Caughey b. Abt 1828, Burgettstown, Washington, PA, d. 12-24-1861, Manchester, Allegheny Co., PA, bur. Union Dale Cemetery, Pittsburgh, Allegheny, PA Div One, Lot 13, Range 4, sec M

> 2-Milton Jay Caughey b. 10-11-1832, Old Allegheny, Allegheny, PA, d. 12-2-1900, Bellevue, Allegheny CO, PA, bur. 12-4-1900, Allegheny Cemetery, Allegheny, PA

> 2-Elizabeth Caughey b. 12-28-1835, Allegheny City, Allegheny, PA, d. 6-3-1923, Pittsburgh, Allegheny, PA, bur. 6-6-1923, Highwood Cemeterty   Pittsburgh, PA

> 2-Anna F. Caughey b. 6-1840, PA, d. 7-9-1919, New Windor, Orange County, NY, bur. Woodlawn Cemetery, Sec M-Lot 127

Children of John and Sarah Jane Harper Caughey

1-John Caughey b. 1-6-1823, Burgettstown, Washington Co., PA, d. 11-7-1904, Haysville, Allegheny Co., PA, bur. 11-9-1904, Sewickley Cemetery, Sewickley, Allegheny, PA Sec F Lot 92 Grave 1

+Sarah Jane Harper b. 1-10-1836, PA, d. 10-21-1914, Sewickley, Allegheny Co., PA, bur. 10-24-1914, Sewickley Cemetery, Sewickley Allegheny, PA Sec F Lot 92 grave 5

2-James Harper Caughey b. 9-2-1856, Allegheny City, Allegheny, .PA, d. 12-24-1873, Pittsburgh, Allegheny, PA, bur. Sewickley Cemetery, Sewickley, Allegheny, PA Sec F Lot 92 Grave #2

2-Clement Patterson Caughey b. 2-19-1859, Allegheny City, Allegheny, PA, d. 11-26-1936, Bellevue, Allegheny, PA, bur. 11-28-1936, Highwood Cemeterty Pittsburgh, PA

2-Robert Coulter Caughey b. 12-31-1861, Allegheny City, Allegheny, .PA, d. 7-21-1951, Los Angeles, CA, bur. Forest Lawn (Glendale) Los Angeles, CA

2-Josephine Odessa Caughey b. 7-29-1864, Allegheny City, Allegheny Co., PA, d. 7-8-1948, Lakewood, Cuyohoga, Ohio, bur. Lakewood Park Cemetery Lakewood, Cuyahoga, Ohio

2-Alice M. Caughey b. 2-16-1867, Allegheny City, Allegheny, PA, d. 1-21-1941, Sewickley, Allegheny Co.PA, bur. Sewickley Cemetery, Sewickley, Allegheny, PA Sec F lot 76 grave #3

2-Jay McIllyer Caughey b. 11-24-1869, Allegheny City, Allegheny, PA, d. 1-14-1945

2-Mary Elizabeth Caughey b. 8-24-1872, Allegheny City, Allegheny, PA, d. 6-26-1967, Veterans Home, Dayton, Ohio, bur. 6-29-1967, Sewickley Cemetery, Sewickley, PA sec F Lot 92 Grave #10

2-John Stevens Caughey b. 4-11-1875, Allegheny City, Allegheny, .PA, d. 10-6-1947, Washington, Washington, PA, bur. 10-9-1947, Sewickley Cemetery, Sewickley, Allegheny, PA Sec F Lot 92 Grave 8

2-Samuel Neal Caughey b. 10-5-1878, Allegheny City, Allegheny, PA, d. 2-16-1959, Middletown, Dauphin, PA, bur. 2-18-1959, Middletown Cemetery, Middletown, Dauphin, PA

Children of John Stevens and Daisy Maude McCormick Caughey

-John Stevens Caughey b. 4-11-1875, Allegheny City , Allegheny, .PA, d. 10-6-1947, Washington, Washington, PA, bur. 10-9-1947, Sewickley Cemetery, Sewickley, Allegheny, PA Sec F Lot 92 Grave 8

-Daisy Maud McCormick b. 8-7-1873, Clarion, Clarion, PA, d. 5-22-1966, Beaver Falls, Beaver, Pa, bur. 5-26-1966, Sewickley Cemetery, Sewickley, Allegheny, PA   Sec F Lot 92 grave 9

2-Robert McCormick Caughey b. 7-6-1902, Old Economy, Beaver, PA, d. 12-8-1929, Haysville, Allegheny, PA., bur. 12-10-1929, Sewickley, PA Sec F Lot 96 grave # 7

2-John StClair Caughey b. 8-7-1904, Old Economy, Beaver PA, d. 2-21-1964, Eustis, Lake County, FL, bur. Wesley Union Cemetery Zanesville, Muskingum, Ohio

2-Richard Stoughton Caughey b. 2-11-1906, Sewickley, Allegheny, PA, d. 2-9-1910, Sewickley, Allegheny, PA, bur. Sewickley, PA Sec F Lot 92 grave #4 unmarked Died of typhoid fever

2-Paul Harper Caughey b. 2-2-1908, Sewickley, Allegheny, PA, d. 11-11-1998, Fairmont , WV, bur. 11-14-1998, Sewickley Cemetery , Sewickley, Allegheny, PA

2-Josephine Lee Caughey b. 7-16-1910, Sewickley, Allegheny, PA, d. 1-18-1911, Sewickley, Allegheny, PA, bur. Sewickley, PA Sec F Lot 92 grave #5 unmarked

2-Daniel Marsh Caughey b. 9-11-1911, Old Economy, PA, d. 4-15-1982, Philadelphia, PA, bur. Sewickley Cemetery, Sewickley, Allegheny, PA

2-Edward Lindsey Caughey b. 11-1-1916, Beaver Street, Sewickley, Allegheny, PA, d. 5-4-2005, Providence County, Burrillville (Pascoag), RI, bur. 7-18-2005, Sewickley Cemetery, Sewickley, Allegheny, PA (sec G lot 38 grave 4)

Descendants of Samuel Neal and Laura McCormick Caughey

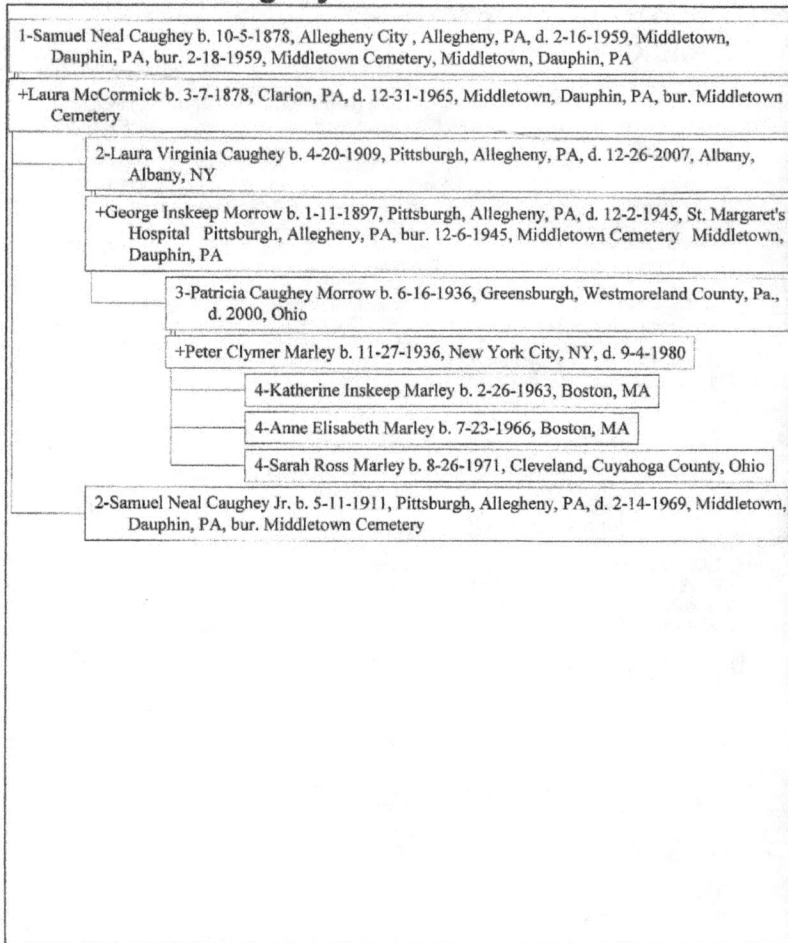

1-Samuel Neal Caughey b. 10-5-1878, Allegheny City , Allegheny, PA, d. 2-16-1959, Middletown, Dauphin, PA, bur. 2-18-1959, Middletown Cemetery, Middletown, Dauphin, PA

+Laura McCormick b. 3-7-1878, Clarion, PA, d. 12-31-1965, Middletown, Dauphin, PA, bur. Middletown Cemetery

    2-Laura Virginia Caughey b. 4-20-1909, Pittsburgh, Allegheny, PA, d. 12-26-2007, Albany, Albany, NY

    +George Inskeep Morrow b. 1-11-1897, Pittsburgh, Allegheny, PA, d. 12-2-1945, St. Margaret's Hospital Pittsburgh, Allegheny, PA, bur. 12-6-1945, Middletown Cemetery Middletown, Dauphin, PA

        3-Patricia Caughey Morrow b. 6-16-1936, Greensburgh, Westmoreland County, Pa., d. 2000, Ohio

        +Peter Clymer Marley b. 11-27-1936, New York City, NY, d. 9-4-1980

            4-Katherine Inskeep Marley b. 2-26-1963, Boston, MA

            4-Anne Elisabeth Marley b. 7-23-1966, Boston, MA

            4-Sarah Ross Marley b. 8-26-1971, Cleveland, Cuyahoga County, Ohio

    2-Samuel Neal Caughey Jr. b. 5-11-1911, Pittsburgh, Allegheny, PA, d. 2-14-1969, Middletown, Dauphin, PA, bur. Middletown Cemetery

Descendants of John St Clair and Sarah "Annie" Shiplett Caughey

1-John StClair Caughey b. 8-7-1904, Old Economy, Beaver PA, d. 2-21-1964, Eustis, Lake County, FL, bur. Wesley Union Cemetery Zanesville, Muskingum, Ohio

+Sarah Animiah "Annie" Shiplett b. 3-22-1906, d. 7-26-1986, bur. Wesley Union Cemetery Zanesville, Ohio

2-John Shiplett Caughey b. 2-13-1924, White Cottage, Muskingum, Ohio, d. 4-24-2008, Zanesville, Muskingum, Ohio

+Jean Audrey Hunt b. 1-9-1925

3-John Stevens Caughey b. 3-16-1948

3-Janet Lynn Caughey b. 8-8-1951, Zanesville, Ohio

+Barry A. Kesslar

2-Richard Bryan Caughey b. 12-3-1928, d. 4-23-2006, Erie, PA

+Susan Ann Kendall b. 1932, d. 5-2006, Westfield, NY

Descendants of Paul Harper and Alice M. Grattan Caughey

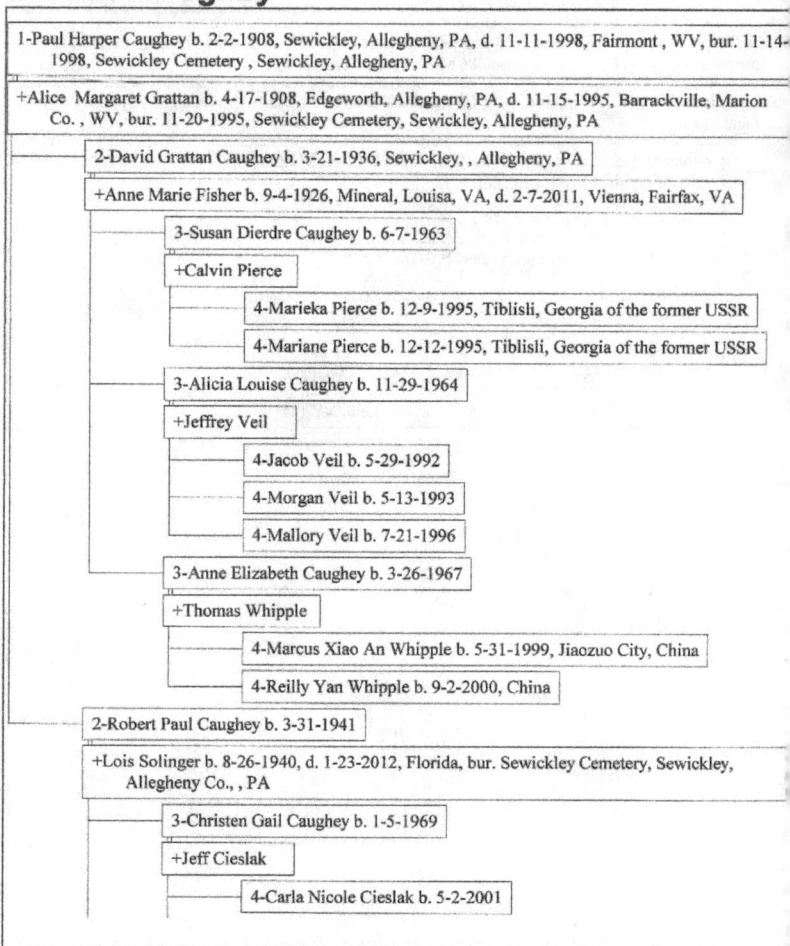

1-Paul Harper Caughey b. 2-2-1908, Sewickley, Allegheny, PA, d. 11-11-1998, Fairmont , WV, bur. 11-14-1998, Sewickley Cemetery , Sewickley, Allegheny, PA

+Alice Margaret Grattan b. 4-17-1908, Edgeworth, Allegheny, PA, d. 11-15-1995, Barrackville, Marion Co. , WV, bur. 11-20-1995, Sewickley Cemetery, Sewickley, Allegheny, PA

2-David Grattan Caughey b. 3-21-1936, Sewickley, , Allegheny, PA

+Anne Marie Fisher b. 9-4-1926, Mineral, Louisa, VA, d. 2-7-2011, Vienna, Fairfax, VA

3-Susan Dierdre Caughey b. 6-7-1963

+Calvin Pierce

4-Marieka Pierce b. 12-9-1995, Tiblisli, Georgia of the former USSR

4-Mariane Pierce b. 12-12-1995, Tiblisli, Georgia of the former USSR

3-Alicia Louise Caughey b. 11-29-1964

+Jeffrey Veil

4-Jacob Veil b. 5-29-1992

4-Morgan Veil b. 5-13-1993

4-Mallory Veil b. 7-21-1996

3-Anne Elizabeth Caughey b. 3-26-1967

+Thomas Whipple

4-Marcus Xiao An Whipple b. 5-31-1999, Jiaozuo City, China

4-Reilly Yan Whipple b. 9-2-2000, China

2-Robert Paul Caughey b. 3-31-1941

+Lois Solinger b. 8-26-1940, d. 1-23-2012, Florida, bur. Sewickley Cemetery, Sewickley, Allegheny Co., , PA

3-Christen Gail Caughey b. 1-5-1969

+Jeff Cieslak

4-Carla Nicole Cieslak b. 5-2-2001

Descendants of Paul Harper and Alice M. Grattan Caughey

- 4-John Robert Cieslak b. 3-15-2003
- 3-Daniel Harper Caughey b. 9-8-1970
- +Catherine Kelly
  - 4-Jillian Quinn Caughey b. 5-12-2003
  - 4-Ryan Harper Caughey b. 8-10-2005
  - 4-Lauren Kelly Caughey b. 8-10-2005

Descendants of Daniel Marsh and Ruth Snodgrass Caughey

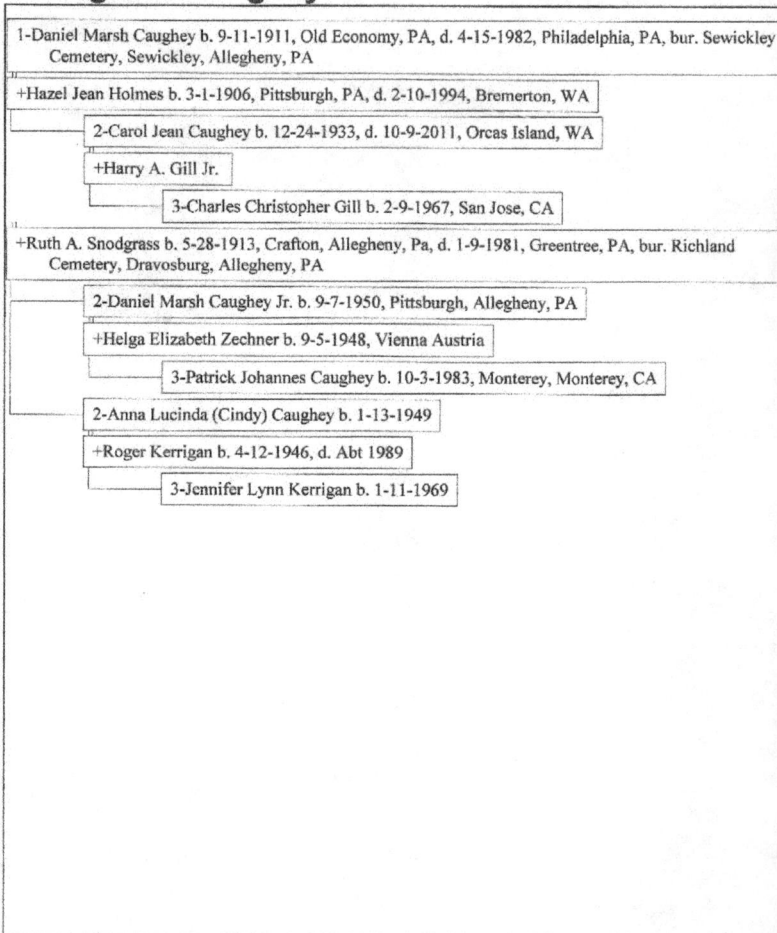

1-Daniel Marsh Caughey b. 9-11-1911, Old Economy, PA, d. 4-15-1982, Philadelphia, PA, bur. Sewickley Cemetery, Sewickley, Allegheny, PA

+Hazel Jean Holmes b. 3-1-1906, Pittsburgh, PA, d. 2-10-1994, Bremerton, WA

    2-Carol Jean Caughey b. 12-24-1933, d. 10-9-2011, Orcas Island, WA

    +Harry A. Gill Jr.

        3-Charles Christopher Gill b. 2-9-1967, San Jose, CA

+Ruth A. Snodgrass b. 5-28-1913, Crafton, Allegheny, Pa, d. 1-9-1981, Greentree, PA, bur. Richland Cemetery, Dravosburg, Allegheny, PA

    2-Daniel Marsh Caughey Jr. b. 9-7-1950, Pittsburgh, Allegheny, PA

    +Helga Elizabeth Zechner b. 9-5-1948, Vienna Austria

        3-Patrick Johannes Caughey b. 10-3-1983, Monterey, Monterey, CA

    2-Anna Lucinda (Cindy) Caughey b. 1-13-1949

    +Roger Kerrigan b. 4-12-1946, d. Abt 1989

        3-Jennifer Lynn Kerrigan b. 1-11-1969

Descendants of Edward L. and Helen A. Mellott Caughey

1-Helen Angeline Mellott b. 7-5-1916, 600 Maplewood Ave., Ambridge, Beaver, PA, d. 5-22-1995, North Providence, Providence County, RI, bur. 5-27-1995, Sewickley Cemetery, Sewickley, Allegheny, PA (Sec G lot 38 grave 5)

+Edward Lindsey Caughey b. 11-1-1916, Beaver Street, Sewickley, Allegheny, PA, d. 5-4-2005, Providence, Providence County, Burrillville (Pascoag), RI, bur. 7-18-2005, Sewickley Cemetery, Sewickley, Allegheny, PA (sec G lot 38 grave 4)

2-Margery Lynne Caughey b. 7-30-1942, Youngstown, Mahoning, Ohio

+Dr. Henry Earle Holden Jr. b. 7-7-1943, Norwich, New London, CT

3-Todd Henry Holden b. 3-14-1971, Danbury, CT

+Trinice Poteete b. 5-22-1973, Rome, GA

4-Robert Henry Holden b. 8-12-2000, Providence, Providence, RI

4-Mark Thomas Holden b. 12-7-2002, Providence, Providence, RI

3-Rebecca Lynne Holden b. 2-3-1973, Westerly, RI

+Darin Roderick Collins b. 3-30-1972, Fort Fairfield, Maine

4-Lance Jarrett Collins b. 2-16-2002, Providence, Providence, RI

4-Isaac Edward Collins b. 3-8-2004, Providence, Providence, RI

+Megan Hughes

+Rev. Phyllis Elizabeth Jennings Hackett b. 6-10-1965, Albany, Albany, NY

2-Robert Edward Caughey b. 6-16-1944, Sewickley, PA

+Dolores Jean Bestwick b. 9-6-1946, Pittsburgh, Allegheny, PA

3-Robert Alan Caughey b. 11-2-1969, Pittsburgh, PA

+Melissa Louise Hite b. 9-17-1967, Alexandria, VA

4-Amanda Caughey b. 8-1-1991, Butler, PA

4-Sean Alan Caughey b. 2-16-1995, Butler, PA

4-Kacee Lynn Caughey b. 5-29-1998, Butler, PA

Descendants of Edward L. and Helen A. Mellott Caughey

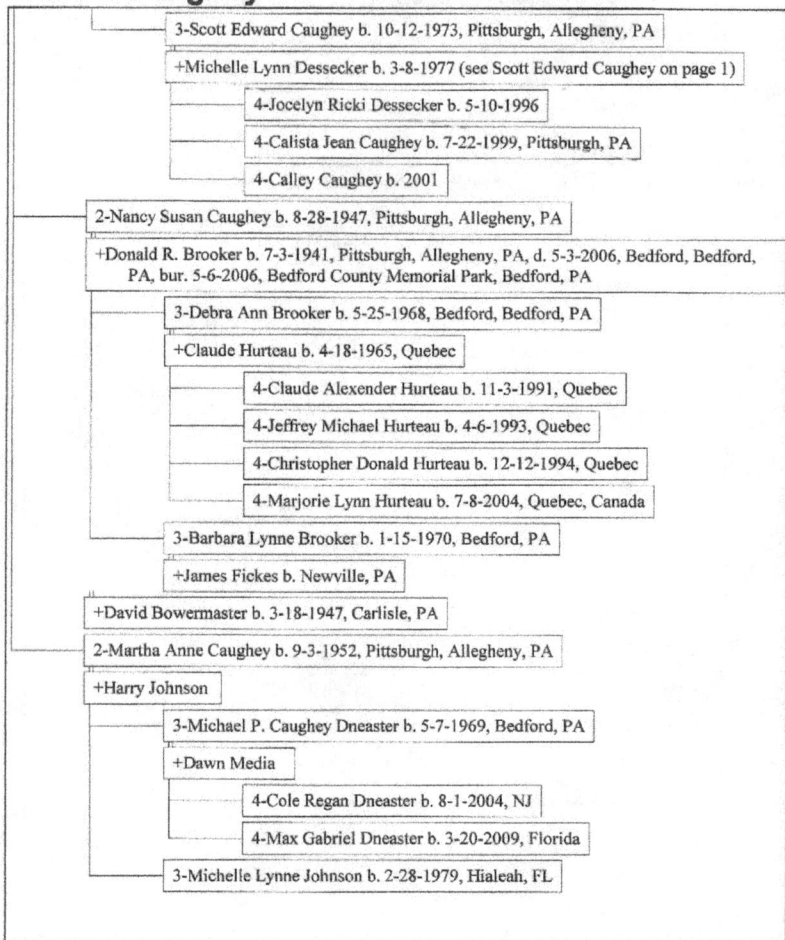

3-Scott Edward Caughey b. 10-12-1973, Pittsburgh, Allegheny, PA

+Michelle Lynn Dessecker b. 3-8-1977 (see Scott Edward Caughey on page 1)

4-Jocelyn Ricki Dessecker b. 5-10-1996

4-Calista Jean Caughey b. 7-22-1999, Pittsburgh, PA

4-Calley Caughey b. 2001

2-Nancy Susan Caughey b. 8-28-1947, Pittsburgh, Allegheny, PA

+Donald R. Brooker b. 7-3-1941, Pittsburgh, Allegheny, PA, d. 5-3-2006, Bedford, Bedford, PA, bur. 5-6-2006, Bedford County Memorial Park, Bedford, PA

3-Debra Ann Brooker b. 5-25-1968, Bedford, Bedford, PA

+Claude Hurteau b. 4-18-1965, Quebec

4-Claude Alexender Hurteau b. 11-3-1991, Quebec

4-Jeffrey Michael Hurteau b. 4-6-1993, Quebec

4-Christopher Donald Hurteau b. 12-12-1994, Quebec

4-Marjorie Lynn Hurteau b. 7-8-2004, Quebec, Canada

3-Barbara Lynne Brooker b. 1-15-1970, Bedford, PA

+James Fickes b. Newville, PA

+David Bowermaster b. 3-18-1947, Carlisle, PA

2-Martha Anne Caughey b. 9-3-1952, Pittsburgh, Allegheny, PA

+Harry Johnson

3-Michael P. Caughey Dneaster b. 5-7-1969, Bedford, PA

+Dawn Media

4-Cole Regan Dneaster b. 8-1-2004, NJ

4-Max Gabriel Dneaster b. 3-20-2009, Florida

3-Michelle Lynne Johnson b. 2-28-1979, Hialeah, FL

Descendants of Edward L. and Helen A. Mellott Caughey

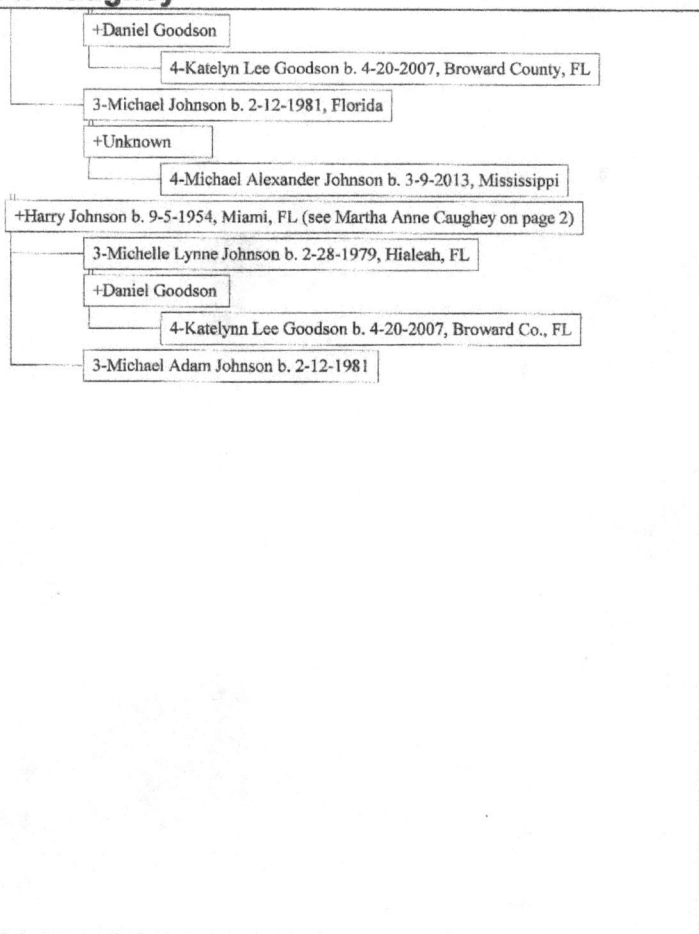

+Daniel Goodson

    4-Katelyn Lee Goodson b. 4-20-2007, Broward County, FL

3-Michael Johnson b. 2-12-1981, Florida

+Unknown

    4-Michael Alexander Johnson b. 3-9-2013, Mississippi

+Harry Johnson b. 9-5-1954, Miami, FL (see Martha Anne Caughey on page 2)

3-Michelle Lynne Johnson b. 2-28-1979, Hialeah, FL

+Daniel Goodson

    4-Katelynn Lee Goodson b. 4-20-2007, Broward Co., FL

3-Michael Adam Johnson b. 2-12-1981

INDEX